100 YEARS
—OF THE—
ROYAL
AIR FORCE

COLIN HIGGS

100 YEARS
—— OF THE ——
ROYAL
AIR FORCE

First published in the UK in 2018

© Demand Media Limited 2018

www.demand-media.co.uk

Content under License to G2 Entertainment Limited

Printed and bound in Europe

ISBN 978-1-78281-326-2

Demand Media Limited, Waterside Chambers, Bridge Barn Lane, Woking,
Surrey, GU21 6NL, United Kingdom.

CONTENTS

INTRODUCTION

During the course of the 20th Century battlefields changed dramatically and it is the aeroplane that created the biggest change of all. This is because the aeroplane can go virtually anywhere unrestrained by sea or land, at any time very quickly and fire weapons of unimagined ferocity and accuracy and gives commanders the perspective of the battlefield only achieved by height.

The Royal Air Force has been central to the evolution of air power and the technologies that have made the aeroplane the decisive weapon of the last 100 years. It is also the oldest independent air force in the world with origins that take it back to the earliest days of powered flight.

Perhaps Britain's most important aircraft of the First World War, the Sopwith Camel was used by day and night, by the RFC, the RAF and the Royal Navy and equipped more than 70 allied squadrons

CHAPTER 1

IN THE BEGINNING

Late in life the Duke of Wellington went on a journey with the author and MP John Wilson Croker. During the journey they tried to guess what kind of terrain they would find over the next hill. Croker expressed surprise at Wellington's success but was told *"Why, I have spent all my life in trying to guess what was at the other side of the hill".* This remark was to become the definition of a commander's need to find out what was happening beyond the range of the naked eye or a pair of binoculars.

Hot air and gas balloons had been used in warfare for decades. Despite early attempts by the Royal Engineers to find a place in the British Army for this basic form of aviation it was not until the Boer War that the balloon made any serious impact.

While balloons were still in their infancy, the army extended development to airships and kites, trying to find some measure of control over position and mobility.

But all changed on a windy December morning in 1903, among the storm-battered dunes of Kittyhawk, North Carolina. Two brothers, Orville and Wilbur Wright, took it in turns to make short powered flights in their

A British military balloon at the siege of Ladysmith during the Boer War in 1899

machine, the Flyer.

With its small light petrol engine and a system of moveable surfaces they didn't just fly the Flyer they controlled its flight.

By 1908 the Wright brothers had already made flights of up to 24 miles. Then they spent a year in Europe try-

Samuel F Cody's wife demonstrating a passenger-lifting kite designed for military use c1906

Cody, to lead the way. Cody had developed man-carrying kites and he had taught kiting to the British army but his real interest lay in powered flight.

In October 1908 his British Army Aeroplane No.1 managed several short flights at Farnborough. Although this and other experiments in powered flight were funded under the auspices of the balloon factory at Farnborough the War Office was not disposed to spend further money. Sceptics who had opposed the development of balloons

ing to sell patents and giving flying demonstrations. They claimed that the aeroplane would make war impossible.

The British military was sceptical so it was left to pioneers like flamboyant American showman, Samuel F.

Kill Devil Hills near Dayton, Ohio. 17 December 1903. Orville Wright makes the first ever recognised powered flight, the start of a revolution

25 July 1909. Louis Bleriot prepares for his ground-breaking flight across the English Channel from the beach near Les Baraques on the French coast

now turned their attention to aircraft and argued that the English Channel removed the need for aerial defence. They also argued that aircraft flew too fast to be of any use when it came to spotting enemy troop movements.

Just five months later Louis Bleriot crossed the channel.

On 26 July 1909, the day after Bleriot's historic flight, a London newspaper, the Daily Graphic, noted that " *When Mr Farman flew a mile it was possible to say that an ingenious toy had been invented. But a machine which can fly from Calais to Dover is not a toy but an instrument of warfare of which soldiers and statesmen must take account.*"

In the following month around 500,000 people saw Europe's aviators competing at the world's first great flying meeting held at Rheims in France.

Among the aircraft on show were monoplanes built by Louis Bleriot. Typical of most aircraft of the period they were made of wood, canvas and wire and flew at about 45mph. Perilously fragile Bleriot's machines were nevertheless successful and would help to equip Britain's Royal Flying Corps at the beginning of the First World War.

With no navigation instruments of any kind pilots often made their way by using landmarks on the ground. With the pilots completely exposed to the elements warm heavy clothing was imperative which meant that there was no lift available to carry guns or bombs. Even so some allowance was made for aircraft. If private enterprise would furnish the machines the government would provide the airfield and facilities.

Mr Charles Rolls, of Rolls Royce, allowed his own Wright aircraft to be used for flying training. When he was

LA BATAILLE DE FLEURUS

Balloon used at the 1794 Battle of Fleurus operated by the French Aerostatic Corps against the Austrian enemy

Since 1900 Germany had been developing giant airships called Zeppelins. Although they were often used to carry passengers over long distances they were also equipping the armed forces. The Home Ports Defence Committee was persuaded that they were vulnerable to attack from airships and that aeroplanes were their best form of defence.

On 1 April 1911 the Air Battalion, Royal Engineers was formed. For the first time the army was prepared to accept that the aeroplane might have a value in wartime as their orders included the job of **"creating a body of expert airmen, organised in such a way as to facilitate the formation of units ready to take the field with troops."** To undertake this role there were just 190 officers, NCOs and other ranks.

In 1911 the French had over 100 aircraft supporting their ground forces with more on order. Germany had 30

killed in July 1910 three artillery officers allowed their own aircraft to take over the job. Despite this assistance, by January 1911 Britain could only boast 57 certified pilots in comparison to 353 French. The British Army did not own a single aircraft while the French forces had 30 with many more on order. However it was airships that made the government change their minds about the use of aircraft.

pilots and 37 machines and they were training for war. By comparison Britain's service was in a sorry state. The army had only 11 qualified airmen, the Royal Navy eight. And all they had was a motley selection of aircraft and two worn out experimental airships. There were monoplanes and biplanes. There were French and British designs with different engines. Each needed slightly differing methods of flying. And every designer had his own refinements to add, making flying training a difficult concept.

In April 1912 the Royal Flying Corps was formed, soon to be followed by the Royal Naval Air Service. Its first commander was Major Frederick Sykes. New designs like the French-built Caudron were ordered as reconnaissance aircraft, a role Sykes was convinced the other services would find useful. Recruits

learnt new trades and skills dedicated to military aviation. For the following three summers this expanding group of men and machines worked to ensure their readiness for war.

August 1909 saw people flock to Rheims in France for the Grand Week of Aviation to watch intrepid aviators from all over the world compete for trophies and glory

CHAPTER 2

GOING TO WAR

Britain went to war in August 1914. Her small, professional expeditionary force of barely 100,000 men took its place on the left of the French lines in Belgium and proved its worth against the advancing German hordes. Amongst their number were 860 members of the RFC and 45 aeroplanes. Within hours two aircraft, a Bleriot monoplane and a BE2, had flown sorties 60 miles ahead of the British army and had brought back useful information on likely routes for the German advance.

The German strategy was to follow the details of the Schlieffen plan which dictated a sweeping attack through Belgium and into Northern France, the encirclement of Paris and a quick end to the war when Paris fell. On 6 September pilots of the RFC noticed that the German army was moving to the north of Paris, across the face of the French lines. This vital and timely information allowed the allies to attack the German flank. The German armies were forced to retreat and the French capital was saved.

For the first time the aircraft had played a key role in changing the face of battle. Armies could no longer assume an element of strategic surprise as their movements could be spotted from the air.

Adolphe Pégoud, test pilot and First World War ace, the first man to fly inverted and loop an aircraft. Seen in 1914 with eight bombs attached to his Bleriot aeroplane

CHAPTER 3

THE KILLING BEGINS

It was supposed to be over by Christmas but instead a war of attrition started with both sides facing each other in trenches across a winter wasteland. Artillery supported by aircraft acting as spotters became one of the most lethal weapons on the battlefield.

Aerial reconnaissance rapidly became essential but to prevent the other side getting back home with information aerial attack was called for. And for the first time domination of the sky assumed military importance.

A fast moving aircraft was very difficult to hit. Then Roland Garros, a French aviator, developed a fixed

Fokker's original interrupter gear, or Stangensteurerung, shown on a 1915 Eindecker

The Fokker M.5K/MG used by Kurt Wintgens, the first fighter pilot to shoot down an enemy aeroplane using synchronised guns in July 1915

German ace Max Immelmann sitting in his Fokker Eindecker in 1915

slow to manoeuvre, were defenceless against the Eindecker and became known as 'Fokker fodder.' The Eindecker scourge of 1915 had begun.

British manufacturers reverted to an old idea, the pusher, which allowed the observer at the front to have an unobstructed field of fire. These 'gun-buses' first flew over the battlefield from February 1916 and helped to end the reign of the Eindecker.

machine gun which fired forwards through the propellor fitted with metal plates to deflect any bullets that struck it. Anthony Fokker improved on Garros' design and created an interrupter gear which only allowed the gun to fire in the split seconds when the propellor was out of the way. The stage was set for the first aircraft designed as a killing machine. The Fokker Eindecker was just that. It was light and manoeuvrable and all the pilot had to do was point his aeroplane at the enemy and press the trigger.

British reconnaissance aircraft such as the BE2, which was very stable but

In July 1916 the allies attacked on the Somme. The RFC struggled to keep up with an ever increasing number and range of missions. Major General Hugh Trenchard, commanding the RFC in France, insisted on continuing the aerial offensive even after the Eindecker Scourge had drained his force.

Fokker E.IV, the final Eindecker, delivered in 1916 but never as successful as previous variants

COUNTERING GERMAN DOMINANCE

The RFC had favoured designs from the Royal Aircraft Factory at the expense of independent manufacturers. To protect their interests the independents grouped together in a move that would soon produce new and better aircraft to equip the squadrons. Three types delivered in 1917 were some of the best aircraft of the war.

The SE5A was undoubtedly the best aircraft to come out of the Royal Aircraft Factory and was popular with pilots because it was stable which made it a good gun platform.

The Bristol F2b was one of the longest serving aircraft in the RFC and later the RAF. It was unusual in being a two seat fighter with two machine guns, one firing forward and another for the observer. It was so successful that the Germans started avoiding combat with the Bristol Fighters.

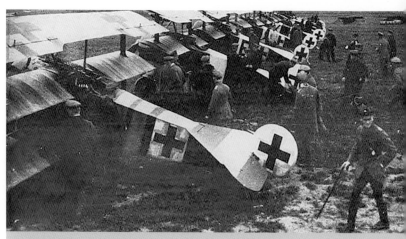

Fokker Triplanes of Jasta 26 based near Erchin in France in the Spring of 1918

The Royal Aircraft Factory's SE5A, their most successful design, on display in 1918 on Horse Guards Parade

Hugely popular at air shows is the Shuttleworth Collections SE5A, F904, built in 1918 and served with 84 Squadron. A rare original airworthy First World War aircraft

The Shuttleworth Collection's Bristol F2b Fighter seen on the flight line at Old Warden in 1967. It is Europe's last airworthy F2b

But possibly the most famous of the three new types was the Sopwith Camel. It was flying by Christmas 1916 and it was a great step forward because it was the first British fighter to have twin synchronised Vickers guns firing forward through the propellor.

Small, tough but immensely manoeuvrable it was fitted with a ferocious rotary engine that could be the downfall of an unsuspecting pilot. In unpracticed hands it could snap into a spin leaving the pilot, in the words of one veteran, with three choices 'Red Cross, Victoria Cross... or wooden cross'.

In experienced hands, though, the Camel was the greatest dogfighter of the war and shot down more enemy aircraft than any other allied fighter. In its heyday it was unmatched by any German fighter save one, the Fokker Triplane. The battle for air supremacy began again.

The Sopwith Camel. In the hands of a skilled pilot the Camel could take on the enemy's best. Credited with the destruction of 1,300 German aircraft

CHAPTER 5

THE AIRCRAFT AS BOMBER

Attacking targets of tactical importance to the army such as artillery, trenches and railways had been a main role of the RFC since the earliest days of the war. However it was the RNAS who pioneered long range bombing to counter the threat of the Zeppelin airships. Germany had seen the potential of aerial bombardment long before the war and the bombs first began to fall on England in 1914.

Their targets were factories vital to the war effort but they were often bombing at night, and from high altitude. Inevitably their bombs often missed causing damage and death among civilians. To calm fears antiaircraft guns were sited around vulnerable factories and squadrons were brought back from France to try and provide some aerial defence. Gradually they began to take a heavy toll on the Zeppelins.

The RNAS had realised earlier in the war that aerial bombardment could extend the ability of the RN to hit

It was the attacks by the German Gotha bombers that terrorised London and other British cities in 1917 and 1918 that helped lead to the formation of the RAF

The Handley Page 0/100 'Bloody Paralyzer' commissioned by the Admiralty, Britain's first purpose-built strategic bomber

strategic targets and seeing Zeppelins as threats to their ships and ports had, as early as 1914 attacked the Zeppelin factory at Friedrichshaven. They only caused slight damage but the effect was dramatic. 4,000 men and anti-aircraft batteries were hastily removed from the Western Front and sent to defend the factory. The RNAS was eager to continue with the bombing of strategic targets and the Admiralty asked Handley Page to build a 'bloody paralyzer' to stop the Germans in their tracks. The result was the HP 0/100 which was gigantic. Its wingspan was 114ft and its powerful twin 250hp engines meant it could carry nearly 1,800lbs of bombs.

The Handley Page 0/400 started to cause real damage in Germany when it came into service in 1918

CHAPTER 6

A UNIFIED FORCE

In 1917 the Germans bombed London using an aircraft flying from France. Air raids on London continued throughout the Summer. Their Gotha bomber could carry just over 1,000 lbs of bombs, not a huge payload but their attacks were so frequent and the defences so inadequate that there was a new public outcry. Parliament acted swiftly by asking the South African statesman, General Jan Smuts, to report. He recommended the setting up of a strengthened unified air force for home defence

He caused uproar by suggesting that *"the day may not be far off when aerial operations with their devastation of enemy lands, and destruction of industrial and populace centres on a vast scale may become the principal operations of war to which the older forms of military and naval operations may become secondary and subordinate."*

Even officers of the RFC and RNAS, including Trenchard, disagreed, not with the proposal itself but that it should be carried out in the middle of a war. However parliament agreed and on 1 April 1918 the Royal Air Force was founded, the first air service in the world that was independent of army or navy.

General Jan Smuts, politician, military commander, member of Britain war cabinet and proponent of the formation of an independent air force

Bristol Fighter ET301 of 22 Squadron RAF preparing for the first ever flight of an RAF aircraft on 1 April 1918

At a stroke the navy lost control of almost 3,000 aircraft and 55,000 officers and naval ratings. They were left with just their shipborne aircraft and even these were to go to the RAF two years later.

At the same time the Independent Force was created to start a bombing offensive against the heartland of Germany on a more massive scale than ever before. In the Spring of 1918 the HP 0/100s were augmented by the even larger 0/400s which could carry the new 1,650lb bomb.

Specifications for even more powerful aircraft were issued, the outcome of which was the Vickers Vimy. Arguably the best of the heavies, the Vimy was delivered just too late to see wartime service. It was smaller than the HP

0/400 but could carry a bomb load of 2,500lbs and carry it faster and further.

At the time of the armistice in November 1918 plans already existed for Vimys to fly 1,000 miles on the round trip from Britain to Berlin. The aircraft would become the standard heavy bomber after the war and it stayed in service on second line duties until the 1930s.

The crew of a Handley Page 0/400 of 207 Squadron, RAF, at Ligescourt near Abbeville in France in August 1918, show off the latest weapon in their armoury, the 1,650lb bomb

CHAPTER 7

THE LAST MONTHS OF WAR

In the Spring of 1918, during the last German offensive of the war on the Marne in France, allied forces found themselves cut off. Desperately short of food and ammunition nothing could get through the sea of mud and so for the first time aircraft of the newly-formed RAF flew over dropping small packages in sandbags to the beleaguered troops. They flew round-the-clock missions and they saved the day. The blockade was broken.

By the Summer of 1918 the new RAF, with more than 20,000 aircraft in service, was the world's strongest air force. Improved supply and design had provided the quality so badly lacking in earlier years and better training was turning out well qualified pilots. However they had one last challenge from the Germans.

The Russian Revolution in 1917 had led to the collapse of the Russian army. allowing the Germans to move troops from Russia to the Western Front. In the Spring of 1918 Germany launched its biggest attack of the war. The RAF found itself in the thick of the fighting flying day and night. On one day alone they shot down 49 enemy aircraft and 6 observation balloons. The German attacks finally ground to a halt in July 1918 and the allies launched the final offensive of the war. As the exhausted Germans retreated the RAF found their targets out in the open rather than in deep trenches. They bombed airfields, bridges, roads and communications, troops were strafed and German aircraft were shot out

A HP 0/400 flown by Lieutenant Kilburn from 216 Squadron, part of 41 Wing based at Ochey in Northern France, crashed on take off with a full bombload late in the war

Just some of the casualties of war. Gassed soldiers from the British 55th (West Lancashire) Division after their stubborn defence of Givenchy during the Battle of Estaires in April 1918

of the sky. The end of the war was near.

On 11 November 1918 the Armistice was signed. The RAF had finally won the air war but at a cost. Losses in one squadron alone, number 80, were appallingly high. In the last 10 months of the war 168 officers were either killed or wounded. In four years of war more than 9,000 men of the RFC, RNAS and RAF had died but the RAF, a service of barely eight months standing, had won the battle in the skies.

Barely 15 years after the Wright Brothers had flown at Kittyhawk the aeroplane had changed the face of war forever.

Crowds in London celebrate the Armistice in November 1918

CHAPTER 8

AN UNEASY PEACE FOR THE RAF

The "war to end all wars" had been costly and over the next few years, the Royal Air Force found itself undermined by lack of investment.

The poster for the 1925 RAF Pageant at Hendon points to the excitement the crowds will feel when they see the RAF's finest on display

Perhaps more than anyone else it was Hugh Trenchard who was key to the survival of the Royal Air Force as an independent force in the years after the First World War

In just two years it was reduced from 399 squadrons and 291,000 personnel to just 41 squadrons and 28,300 personnel. The demise of the RAF seemed certain.

However the increasing popularity of public air displays allowed the RAF to demonstrate that taxpayers money was being well spent.

RAF commander Air Marshal Sir Hugh Trenchard was quick to realise

The Vickers Vimy of John Alcock and Arthur Whitten Brown crashed in a bog at Clifden, Co. Galway after their record breaking transatlantc flight in June 1919

the value of this publicity and he encouraged squadrons to form their own display teams.

Each year, a different squadron was nominated as the official RAF team.

The first Hendon RAF Pageant took place in 1922, in front of more than 60,000 people. It quickly became an important annual event and each year crowds flocked to watch formation flying and aerobatic feats performed in the very same aircraft that had helped to win the war.

The Hendon air show rapidly became a part of the Summer season which meant there were many in the

Ross and Keith Smith, Australian brothers who flew from Britain to Australia in November 1919

Captured German battleship, the Ostfriesland, sunk by aerial bombing during air power trials in July 1921

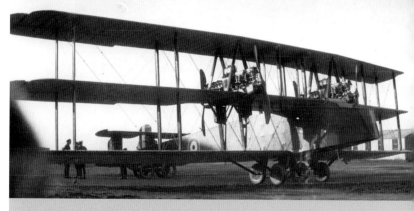

The Bristol Braemar was one of the heavy bomber prototypes cancelled at the end of the war. It was designed to carry almost two thirds of a ton of bombs all the way to Berlin

General Giulio Douhet, Italian air power theorist and advocate of strategic bombing much admired by Trenchard and Mitchell

crowd not without influence.

Record-breaking flights were another way to fire the public imagination. The RAF's determination, and ability, to fly further, faster and higher than anyone else was demonstrated many times between the wars.

In June 1919 John Alcock, a recently demobbed RAF pilot, and Arthur Whitten Brown, an ex-RAF Observer, flying a Vimy, achieved what had seemed to be impossible - they bridged the Atlantic by air!

Then in November of the same year, and also in a Vimy, Ross and Keith Smith, flew from Hounslow near London to Australia in under 28 days, the longest flight the world had ever seen.

Flights like these did more than just raise the profile of the RAF. They also forced military strategists to think long and hard about the use of air power in future conflicts. And the bomber was central to their ideas.

The belief was that bombers could be used to attack strategic targets that would take an enemy out of the war. The UK didn't buy a fighter force at the time based on the view that to find a bomber force coming to attack a target was almost impossible. Therefore it was believed that it was impossible to stop an enemy bomber force from attacking your critical targets which led to Prime Minister Stanley Baldwin's comment that 'the bomber will always get through'.

Trenchard had become an ardent believer in the potency of the bomber, a belief reinforced by the writing of the Italian theorist General Giulio Douhet.

He foresaw how, in future conflicts, aircraft could *"go far behind the fortified lines of defence without breaking through them. The battlefield will be limited only by the boundaries of the nations at war, and all of their citizens will become combatants, since all of them will be exposed to the aerial offensives of the enemy. There will be no distinction any longer between soldiers and civilians."*

Trenchard warmed to Douhet's theories. But the First Sea Lord, Admiral Beatty, wasn't so easily convinced. He threatened to resign unless the Navy got its air force back. Trenchard's response was uncompromising *"It is on the bomber that we must rely for defence. It is on the destruction of enemy industries, and above all, on the lowering of morale caused by bombing that ultimate victory rests."*

Beatty had good reason to be wary of air power. American General Billy Mitchell had already bombed and sunk the captured German battleship, the Ostfriesland, to demonstrate dramatically that air power was challenging the role of the navy as the defender of a nation's strategic interests.

General Billy Mitchell showed the practical use of aerial bombing with the sinking of the Ostrfriesland

CHAPTER 9

MARITIME COMMITMENT

For almost 20 years from 1918 the Royal Navy made repeated attempts to regain control over their aircraft. They seemed to be getting somewhere in 1924 when the Fleet Air Arm of the RAF was formed. It was agreed that so-called 'fleet flights', normally controlled by the RAF, would be given over to the navy when they were flown from aircraft carriers. Apart from

Sir Samuel Hoare, Secretary of State for Air, ready to inspect the RAF's new Supermarine Southampton maritime reconnaissance flying boat at Cromer in 1925

The five RAF Southamptons from 204 Squadron take off from Mount Batten in Plymouth in 1932 for their Mediterranean 'cruise' to Malta

this maritime aviation suffered from government under funding always losing out to the bombers. There were, of course, some new maritime aircraft. The Supermarine Southampton virtually saved the concept of the flying boat from extinction after a number of expensive failures.

Its day to day role was the reconnaissance of Britain's coastline but it became more famous for its long distance flights. In 1927 four Southamp-

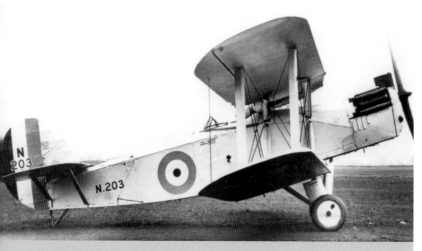

The Blackburn Ripon torpedo bomber prototype N203 first flew in 1

One of only five Blackburn Iris long range flying boats ever built that equipped 209 Squadron from 1930. This aircraft, S1263, sank after a collision at Plymouth on 12 January 1933

tons went on a flag-waving 27,000 mile trip around the Mediterranean and the Far East. Blackburn was another major supplier of flying boats. The Iris was an enormous three engined flying boat with a range of up to 500 miles. It had all the comforts of home with sleeping accommodation, a kitchen and a canteen for the crew while on long range reconnaissance missions.

Blackburn also built a number of land or carrier-based torpedo bombers for the fleet flights. The Dart was the first entering service in 1923. Its top speed was only 107 mph but its landing speed of around 38 mph made it a natural choice for aircraft carrier use. The Ripon, introduced in 1929, was the natural successor to the Dart and it set the standard for torpedo bombers until

the arrival of the Beaufort in 1939.

The full lack of maritime development can be seen by the fact that the Fairey Swordfish, which became the standard torpedo bomber of the Fleet Air Arm in 1936, had a performance little better than that of the Ripon.

Finally in 1934 defence expenditure began to increase but as priorities moved backwards and forwards between bombers and fighters naval requirements tended to get lost in the rush. In 1936, as part of a wholesale restructuring of RAF organisation, the old Coastal Area was renamed as Coastal Command. Only one area saw any expansion and that was the Fleet Air Arm. The rest of the command had to struggle on with its obsolete biplanes.

Air Chief Marshal Sir Hugh Trenchard inspects engineering apprentices of No.1 School of Technical Training at Halton at their passing out parade

CHAPTER 10

TRAINING

Of course aircraft were only part of the story. As Trenchard knew only too well an air force needs highly skilled people to run it. In creating its own training systems, the RAF was also developing its own traditions and infrastructure as an independent air service. Trenchard surmised correctly that the more strongly it became established the harder it would be for it to disband.

Cranwell, originally a training base for the Royal Naval Air Service, became the site for a new RAF cadet college. Halton Park was where engineering apprentices were trained and an RAF Staff College was set up at Andover, later to move to Bracknell.

By 1922 these 3 institutions were up and running providing a regular flow of well-trained officers, riggers,

A growing RAF Cranwell cadet college seen from an Avro 504N training aircraft

Avro 504K E3269 of No.2 Flying Training School probably at RAF Duxford in 1923

fitters and all the other trades that were essential to the smooth running of the service.

Trenchard also introduced short service commissions so that there would be a pool of trained pilots in civilian life who could be called up in the event of war.

To extend their continued association with the RAF he created Special Reserve squadrons.

And the Auxiliary Air Force was formed to give weekend flyers a taste of the service.

In order to ensure the pilots got the best training possible he established a Central Flying School. Much of the training was on the Avro 504, commissioned by the Admiralty and first flown in 1913 as a reconnaissance and light bomber in the First World War.

CHAPTER 11

POLICING THE EMPIRE

Potentially fatal cuts in the RAF's budget could not be avoided solely by flying demonstrations. Practical examples of the RAF's effectiveness were required and the Empire provided the opportunity needed.

Air units had been operating in the far flung corners of the Empire since 1915. But after the war the potential for the RAF to undertake policing duties at a fraction of the cost of military garrisons became obvious.

Throughout India and the Middle East, the presence of the RAF steadily grew until policing duties became the sole preserve of the RAF, flying aircraft like the Bristol Fighter, a veteran of the First World War, well into the 1920s.

In December, 1919 Trenchard wrote *"it is perhaps not too much to hope that before long it will prove possible to regard the Royal Air Force units not as an addition to the military garrison but as a substitute for it."*

An Airco DH9A of 27 Squadron based at RAF Risalpur flies over the North West Frontier of India in the early 1920s

Bristol F2b of 5 Squadron flying from its base at RAF Quetta in India. The squadron flew these ageing aircraft right through until 1931

Two Bristol F2bs of 5 Squadron flying over the majestic scenery of Northern India in the 1920s

Time and again the RAF demonstrated the potency of aircraft quelling tribal insurrections. They could fly over deserts and mountains, drop a bomb and be back at base in time for tea. These same operations would have taken the army weeks, if not months, to complete on foot. The immense savings were just what the treasury wanted.

After one such rebellion in Somaliland Leopold Amery, the Colonial Secretary, said: *"All was over in three weeks. The total cost worked out at £77,000, the cheapest war in history."*

At the Cairo conference in March 1921 Trenchard's confidence in the RAF received official support. It was given the lion's share of the responsibility for the defence of the Middle East territories, although India stayed under the army's command .

The conduct of the air war in the Middle East and India was far removed from the reality of a major conflict. There were no factories or transportation lines to attack, just villages, crops and livestock. And aircraft always dropped leaflets to warn villagers of a forthcoming attack .

It was no life of luxury for the RAF pilots and crew. Almost always the terrain was desert or mountain. The nights were freezing; the daytime temperatures as high as 50 degrees centigrade.

The Vickers Victoria was one of the first new post-war aircraft. A troop carrier and general transport it equipped two squadrons in Egypt and Iraq, maintaining communications all over the Empire

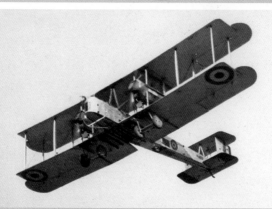

The Vickers Vimy was too late to see service during the war but was put to good use both as bomber and airmail carrier in Iraq and Egypt during the 1920s

But the pilots and ground crew still needed supplies - which had to come in to these far-flung bases by air. Fortunately, at the end of the war, the RAF had a large number of heavy bombers surplus to requirements. Many of them were Vickers Vimys which were now scheduled for the scrap heap. Vimys made great transport aircraft, plying the Middle East routes delivering mail and stores and, when used as troop carriers, they got their passengers to their destinations in days, rather than weeks.

Finally, in the late twenties, units started to receive replacements for their worn-out aircraft. First to arrive was the Westland Wapiti which soon became one of the most ubiquitous aircraft flown by the RAF in the inter-war period.

The second to arrive was the Hawker Hart, the first of a long line of graceful Hawker aircraft that would encompass almost every role required of the RAF. Designed by Sydney Camm, the Hart was the fastest aircraft in the RAF at the time. Embarrassingly, this day bomber was even faster than the current fighters.

The Hawker Hart was deployed as a light bomber throughout the Middle East and India during the 1930s

CHAPTER 12

TRENCHARD RETIRES

Trenchard retired on 1 January 1930 after more than 10 years of fighting for the future of the RAF

He had fought his battles in government and in the furthest reaches of the Empire, and he had won. He had created an ethos for his service and now it was at the forefront of military thinking for the future. But most of all he had set a standard of professionalism and independence that remains with the RAF to this day.

Hugh Trenchard retired in 1930 following 37 years of service with the British Army, Royal Flying Corps and Royal Air Force

CHAPTER 13

MODERNISING FOR WAR

In spite of a lack of orders from the RAF one particular designer was pushing the boundaries of air speed through the development of an aircraft intended not to win wars but to win an air race

Air racing had become big box office and international competitions offered impressive prizes and the possibilities of commercial success. The most coveted award was the Schneider trophy. Three wins in a row and you won it outright.

Supermarine was a small seaplane manufacturer based near Southampton. In 1922, the Supermarine Sea Lion II and her RAF crew won the Schneider Trophy for the first time with a speed of over 120mph. In 1927 Supermarine entered the first of their S series monoplane seaplanes designed by their chief designer, RJ Mitchell. Britain won that year and again in 1929. In 1931 a team flying an S6B won again. Now, the Schneider Trophy would belong to Britain forever.

On the same day another S6B also

Two Supermarine S6Bs and a single S6A prepared for the 1931 Schneider Trophy race at Calshot in Hampshire

gained the absolute world speed record at just over 379 mph. RAF commanders were shattered to realise that a privately built aircraft could fly 170 mph faster than the Hawker Fury - their latest and fastest operational aircraft..

The Schneider Trophy success inspired Mitchell to enter a design for an Air Ministry specification for a new monoplane fighter. The result was the legendary Supermarine Spitfire.

By 1934 it was slowly dawning on the government that something had to be done about air defences

In the early years of the century the position of the Royal Navy was unassailable. It had been instrumental in building and preserving the British Empire but now the country was at risk from attack from the air. In fact all the fighting services were seriously underfunded and underequipped.

The reason for this went back to 1919 when the Treasury had instituted the Ten Year Rule. This restricted expenditure on military matters for ten years on the assumption it would take at least ten years for a potential aggressor to build up sufficient forces to be a threat. There would therefore be plenty of time to re-equip. Unfortunately this optimistic rule was extended year by year until by 1932 obsolete biplane designs like the Handley Page Heyford and Fairey Gordon bombers with open cockpits and fixed undercarriages were still providing the backbone of the RAF.

Sir John Salmond had taken over from Hugh Trenchard as Chief of the Air Staff in 1930. It was a time of great economic depression. There were calls for disarmament and even suggestions that bombing should be banned altogether. What's more the great proportion of Salmond's squadrons were stationed overseas leaving him little or no scope for the improvement of British air defences. Events unfolding in Europe finally made this vulnerability apparent.

A Supermarine magazine advertisement proudly showing their record in the Schneider Trophy races of 1922, 1927 and 1929

Two of the stop-gap bombers built for the 1930s RAF. The Fairey Gordon of 40 Squadron (top) and Handley Page Heyford (bottom) were both replaced just in time for the outbreak of war in 1939

CHAPTER 14

THE ROAD TO WAR

By the mid '30s, both Germany and Italy had begun building-up huge armed forces in flagrant breach of the Versailles Treaty.

Britain's initial response was to instigate a programme that would expand its military capabilities including the development of new bomber types in the vain hope of deterring Germany's ambition. Three manufacturers successfully tendered new bomber designs. Armstrong Whitworth were to build the Whitley, Handley Page the Hampden but the best known, and the aircraft that was to give the longest service of the three was the Vickers Wellington. Over 11,000 of these were to be built. The aircraft was based on Barnes Wallis' geodetic design and was to prove extremely resilient to the ravages of anti aircraft fire. Hundreds were to return from bombing raids with half their fuselage ripped to shreds. But even before these aircraft

The Treaty of Versailles signed in 1919 infuriated and impoverished the German people so perhaps there was no surprise when Hitler came to power vowing to rebuild Germany

A display of air power. This gathering of the Luftwaffe in Budapest in June 1937 showed their growing might with Me109 fighters and Ju52 transports in attandance

had been delivered Britain's priorities had changed.

The struggle to modernise the RAF took on a new urgency when the Luftwaffe's Condor Legion unleashed a murderous onslaught on civilians in the Spanish Civil War, bombing and slaughtering indiscriminately.

The Legion was equipped with the Luftwaffe's latest aircraft and the crews relished their first taste of combat. The Nazi war machine was getting valuable experience.

The Handley Page Hampden was one of the first of the new generation of bombers that equipped the RAF at the outbreak of war

Proving its worth during the Spanish Civil War the Ju87 Stuka dive bomber caused terror and destruction across Europe in 1939 and 40

The Armstrong Whitworth Whitley was an integral part of Bomber Command from 1937

The issue of Britain's air defence was finally addressed by the government. Sir Thomas Inskipp reported in 1937 that more fighters should be built and more importantly should have priority over the bombers.

Orders were to be concentrated on a few types such as RJ Mitchell's Spitfire. It would become the most famous aircraft in the RAF's history

The RAF was finally modernising for war.

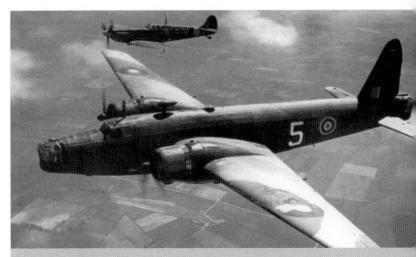

More than 11,000 Vickers Wellingtons were built and served the RAF throughout the Second World War in numerous roles

CHAPTER 15

RECRUITING FOR WAR

This expansion required a new structure for the RAF, one which took aircraft types and their roles into consideration. Therefore Bomber, Fighter and Coastal Commands were created. A new training command was also set up to cope with the huge influx of new recruits.

At the same time the RAF set up a volunteer reserve encouraging young men to train as pilots, observers or wireless operators. Such was the success of the scheme that when war finally came more than 10,000 reservists were ready and raring to go. But they still needed a huge influx of trained aircrew and many came from Britain's Dominions and allies, Australia, New Zealand, South Af-

rica, Rhodesia and Canada.

Between 1934 and late 1939 the personnel strength more than tripled. The number of operational aircraft quadrupled to over 3,200 and the number of airfields rose from 52 to 89.

Three of the key men responsible for the growth of the RAF. Cyril Newall (left) Chief of the Air Staff, James Robb (centre) CO of CFS and Charles Burnett (right), AOCinC Training Command with HM King George VI in May 1938

CHAPTER 16

FIGHTER COMMAND AT WAR

The Spitfire prototype first flew on 5 March 1936. Its performance was so outstanding that the RAF immediately ordered 310. However it didn't get into RAF hands for two years. Basic production problems were mainly to blame. Supermarine had been building aircraft for many years but only in wood. Working with metal proved to be a very different and difficult task.

Both Supermarine and their sub-contractors were accustomed to building small quantities of aircraft at a time. Now mass production called on them to learn new skills and disciplines - something which would hit many aircraft manufacturers before the end of the war.

But the years of frantic activity were now beginning to pay off. Finally the new fighters began to arrive. By the

Vickers-Supermarine Spitfire prototype K5054 shown in April 1936 soon after the first flight

This Spitfire Mk.1 of 19 Squadron at Duxford in 1938 was the ninth production aircraft

outbreak of war a total of nine squadrons were equipped with Spitfires. The Hawker Hurricane had arrived the previous year and made up a further 15 squadrons.

The factories were working at full speed. No-one was sure whether they could produce enough aircraft in the time that was left.

But very soon they would know for certain.

The Hawker Hurricane prototype K5083 flew for the first time on 6 November 1935

CHAPTER 17

THE BATTLE OF BRITAIN

Famously the Spitfire's finest hour was the Battle of Britain. In the Battle for France the RAF had lost many experienced pilots in the face of an overwhelming German force. Now invasion threatened Britain but first the Luftwaffe had to win the air battle.

The defence of Britain was in the hands of a small band of young pilots. They were under the command of

Air Chief-Marshal Sir Hugh Dowding, CinC Fighter Command between 1936 and 1940

A German map showing their understanding of the British radar network in 1940

Air Marshal Sir Hugh Dowding who knew something of the new technology required to modernise the RAF during the 1930s. Under Dowding the RAF set up the first integrated defence system combining radar and wireless communications with the new fighters now equipping the squadrons. As soon as enemy aircraft formations were

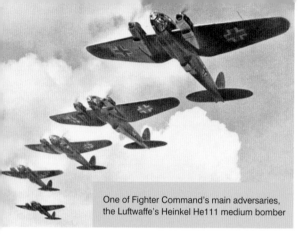

One of Fighter Command's main adversaries, the Luftwaffe's Heinkel He111 medium bomber

spotted by radar or the Observer Corps the information was passed to a central control room at Fighter Command headquarters. This information was then passed to the group operations room and on to the nearest sector station. Squadrons would scramble already knowing in which direction the enemy were heading and the strength of their force.

Until 1940 this was the theory. And then the Germans attacked. The success of their assaults on Poland and France was largely due to the Luftwaffe destroying the opposing air forces on the ground. Once again the German targets were

A Hawker Hurricane being refuelled during the Battle of Britain in 1940

A vital part of Britain's home defence network was the Royal Observer Corps. Perched on a rooftop within sight of St Paul's Cathedral an observer searched for enemy aircraft

A regular sight in the early weeks of the Battle of Britain. An RAF fighter station comes under attack

Perhaps the public face of the Battle of Britain. Hurricane pilots of 56 Squadron, including famous New Zealander ace Colin Gray, relax and joke in a quiet moment at RAF North Weald in the Summer of 1940

Pilots and crew from 264 Squadron in front of the squadron leader's Boulton Paul Defiant fighter in 1940

radar stations and airfields. Time and again RAF squadrons scrambled as huge enemy formations of bombers escorted by Messerschmitt fighters headed towards Britain. Spitfire pilots used their greater manoeuvrability to draw the fighter escorts away from the bombers leaving the Hurricanes to attack them.

But Fighter Command was suffering. Although the British fighters had the advantage of being able to land, refuel and rearm quickly constant attacks on airfields had pushed fighters further away from the combat areas in the south east. Reinforcements from 12 Group north of the Thames were taking too long to fly into the battle. Losses were being sustained at an unacceptable rate but then Fighter Command got a much needed respite. On 25 Aug 1940 Bomber Command launched an attack on Berlin. In retaliation Hitler ordered the Luftwaffe to stop their attacks on

airfields and instead launch an all out blitz on London. Fighter Command was able to regroup and continue to engage the enemy aircraft. Luftwaffe losses mounted. By the middle of September, in order to reduce their losses, they switched to night attacks. In truth the Luftwaffe had already lost the Battle of Britain and the invasion of Britain was postponed indefinitely.

"NEVER WAS SO MUCH OWED BY SO MANY TO SO FEW"
THE PRIME MINISTER

One of the most famous images of the Battle of Britain, the poster with Winston Churchill's words of thanks to Fighter Command

CHAPTER 18

THE RAF STRIKES BACK

Fighter Command could be justly proud of its victory and in 1941 went on the offensive. Raids known as circuses, rodeos and rhubarbs were mounted to entice Luftwaffe fighters into the air where they could be pounced on by swarms of Spitfires

Initially MkV Spitfires were used but now the Luftwaffe had improved versions of the Messerschmitt 109. They also had a totally new aircraft that began to outfly the RAF fighters, the Focke Wulf 190. Something had to be done and that was the Mk.IX Spitfire.

Introduced in May 1942, supposedly as a stopgap, the Mk.IX had a speed in excess of 400mph. With two machine guns and two 20mm cannon it proved

After suffering heavy losses as a day fighter the Defiant proved its worth as a night fighter. Here are Defiants of 264 Squadron from West Malling in 1941

The Bristol Beaufighter proved to be a very successful aircraft in so many roles and in all theatres of war

The Spitfire V was a marked improvement when it came into service in 1941. Here Mk.Vs await testing or ferrying at the Castle Bromwich factory

Similarly the Hurricane was being upgraded. This Mk.IID is fitted with 3inch rockets on rails and a tropical filter making it suitable for use in North Africa or the Far East

so successful that it stayed in service until the end of the war.

At the same time Fighter Command aircraft were dealing with night raids on British cities.

The Boulton Paul Defiant, an aircraft that had proved to be totally unsuitable as a day fighter, adapted well to night fighting. But it was the Beaufighter, with its integral radar system, that finally began to gain the upper hand at night. In the European theatre RAF fighters and pilots had found new levels of effectiveness at air to air combat.

The Gloster Gladiator provided sterling service specially in the Mediterranean during 1940 and 41. Here is Sea Gladiator N5520, nicknamed 'Faith' which helped to defend Malta

2,000 miles away in North Africa the idea of using these powerful aircraft to attack the enemy on the ground was finding favour. Earlier in the war the Germans had used Stuka dive bombers to great effect. Their ability to drop a bomb on moving targets such as tanks was immensely useful to the army. The Western Desert Air Force was equipped with Hurricanes that had gradually been outclassed by the new German fighters. But equipped with rockets and 40mm anti tank cannon the Hurricane's extremely strong airframe made it the ideal ground attack aircraft.

These 'Hurribombers' helped turn the tide of the war in North Africa and caused havoc along the congested coast road attacking the German Afrika Korps and destroying tanks and trucks with their powerful cannon. Often the enemy was only a few hundred yards away from friendly forces and it was up to the ground troops to give pinpoint locations for the targets. In the event this ground to air co-operation proved itself time and again.

On Malta the Western Desert Air Force was desperately engaged in a battle to keep the Mediterranean sea lanes open. Here there were no sophisticated multi-role fighters available. Instead the Gloster Gladiator, the last biplane fighter in the RAF, equipped many squadrons and although it was one of the fastest biplanes ever built it was no match for the new generation of German monoplanes.

Even so three historic Gladiators, christened Faith, Hope and Charity, defended the island against overwhelming odds until modern replacements arrived.

CHAPTER 19

THE MOSQUITO ARRIVES

The Mosquito was developed privately by the De Havilland company without any particular role in mind. But it answered perfectly the RAF's need for a dedicated force of fighter bombers. The Mosquito was very versatile and devastatingly effective. The fighter bomber variants boasted armaments combining 20mm cannon, machine guns and 60lb rockets as well as still being able to carry up to 500lb of bombs. The Mosquito was powered by two Rolls Royce Merlin engines which gave it a top speed of 415 mph, enough to outrun all of the enemy fighters of the day. And its all-wooden construction meant it was virtually invisible to radar.

De Havilland Mosquito prototype E0234 at Hatfield on 27 November 1940 before its first flight

The De Havilland Mosquito FB.VI was the most numerous of the type and was designed as a fighter-bomber. However it was used in many roles using cannon, machine guns, bombs and rockets

As the planning for the allied invasion of France developed Number 2 Tactical Air Force was formed. It was given the task of winning air superiority so that the troops could land on the beaches unmolested by German aircraft.

Virtually everything of importance was attacked. Boats, trains and vehicles as well as the bridges, tunnels and railways on which they tried to move. German aircraft were destroyed before they could even get airborne.

June 6 1944 was the longest day, D-Day, when allied forces invaded Western Europe. 2,000 RAF fighters played a major role in the largest aerial umbrella ever assembled. But the expected Luftwaffe counter attacks never materialised. Not only had they been badly depleted by constant attacks in recent months but Hitler's insistence that the allied attack would come at the

Pas de Calais meant that the bulk of the Luftwaffe's remaining aircraft was nowhere near the invasion area.

Allied air superiority was so great that they flew over 14,000 sorties on D-Day while the Luftwaffe managed less than 700. Throughout the day close co-operation between ground and air ensured that if anything German moved it was instantly attacked. The beaches were virtually cut off from German reinforcements and within days allied aircraft began operating from captured airfields in Normandy.

But the fighter bombers' greatest triumph was still to come. At the beginning of August the allies finally broke out of the Normandy bridge-head threatening to trap thousands of German troops and tanks in a pocket near Falaise. As the German troops tried to escape both ends of the pocket

Hawker's next venture after the Hurricane was the Typhoon. Here is a Mk.Ib of 197 Squadron in 1944

were attacked by rocket firing aircraft, Typhoons, Tempests and American Thunderbolts, causing mayhem among the trapped Germans. Aircraft were allocated 'kill boxes', areas of ground that were constantly patrolled. Anything that moved was destroyed.

More than 10,000 Germans died in the hell of the Falaise pocket.

Now the allies swept through France and Belgium with the fighters trying to keep pace moving from airfield to airfield, sometimes staying for just a few days. Close air support was now being run with total efficiency. The 'cab rank' system ensured that there were always plenty of rocket-firing aircraft on call to ground troops to deal with stubborn German defences.

Bombing raids by allied aircraft continued throughout 1944, their effectiveness boosted by the arrival of the Mk.III Mustang. Although made in America this aircraft was originally commissioned by the RAF as an advanced fighter. When it was eventually given the same Merlin engines as the Spitfire it became one of the fastest aircraft of the war and, most importantly, it had a flying range of up to 750 miles. Allied bombers could now be escorted by Mustangs all the way to their targets over Europe and home again. But Germany could still hit back in other ways.

On June 13 1944 the first wave of a new terror hit London, the V1 flying bombs. These primitive cruise missiles came in at 400mph, not an easy target for ground defences, but at nearly 450mph Tempests could outpace them and shoot them down.

In the last months of the war Fighter Command enjoyed total air supremacy, the battle with the Luftwaffe won.

A North American Mustang III of 19 Squadron, the aircraft which revolutionised escort duties for the bomber streams

An example of the damage caused in London by V.1 flying bombs. No wonder the launch sites in France became prime targets

CHAPTER 20

BOMBER COMMAND AT WAR

By 1939 Bomber Command was rapidly expanding with aircraft such as the Wellington in readiness to stop the Nazis in their tracks. However many pilots were still being trained in Hind biplanes and the lack of enough modern aircraft meant that on the outbreak of war 17 out of the 55 squadrons that formed the front line had to be withdrawn to train new recruits.

Vickers Wellington Mk.III of 419 Squadron RCAF operating in early 1942

A Bristol Blenheim Mk.I of 90 Squadron Bomber Command pictured just before the outbreak of war

When war was declared Bomber Command went on the offensive from the first days. Small groups of twin-engined bombers unprotected by friendly fighters flew in broad daylight to attack German shipping and naval installations. The Bristol Blenheim light bombers, in particular, made easy targets for the Luftwaffe.

During the Battle of France, in May 1940, the British bomber force was decimated. Even worse than the loss of aircraft was the dreadful loss of well-trained pilots whose experience would be sorely missed in the battles to come.

However Bomber Command continued the offensive during 1940 by concentrating many of their attacks on the French ports holding German invasion barges.

At the same time they were receiving a long stream of contradictory orders.

Air Marshal Sir Arthur Harris was made AOCinC of Bomber Command in 1942, one of the most influential RAF appointments during the war

The navy wanted them to bomb ships, the army wanted them to bomb tank factories. Nobody could agree what targets they should hit.

1942 was a vital year for the whole future of Bomber Command and its strategic offensive. Air Marshal Sir Arthur Harris was appointed its new commander in chief. He was a natural leader who's force of personality brought respect and dedication from all ranks.

He had a paltry force of about 500 bombers of which no more than 250 were serviceable at any one time. And his experience at group level had taught

him that precision bombing with large formations of aircraft was simply not possible. His views were backed up by a report prepared in the Autumn of 1941. It concluded that only eight per cent of aircraft on previous raids had actually bombed within a 75 square mile area round the target.

Also the growing strength of German night fighters and anti-aircraft batteries made the job hazardous in the extreme. To cap it all losses on previous operations had left the command woefully short of trained crews. But the bomber offensive had to continue.

CHAPTER 21

FOUR-ENGINED HEAVIES

The equipment situation was already being improved by the delivery of four engined heavy bombers with greater range and bomb load. Handley Page delivered the very successful Halifax which began operations in 1941. However it was the Avro Lancaster which was undoubtedly the finest bomber of the war. It had a normal payload of 14,000 lbs, three times the load of a Wellington, and could be adapted to carry the enor-

When the Handley Page Halifax Mk.I went on operations from March 1941 it was not perfect but a massive improvement over previous Bomber Command aircraft

mous 22,000lb Grand Slam bomb. It had the range to penetrate deep into enemy territory and attack targets that had previously been unreachable and its Merlin 20 engines gave it enviable speed and reliability.

The Lancaster's baptism of fire was a raid on Augsburg on 17 April 1942.

The target was the MAN diesel engine factory where submarine engines were built. Starving the U-boat force of new engines was the main reason for the raid but Harris also wanted to show Bomber Command's capabilities. It was the first deep penetration raid into Germany, a 1,000 mile round trip, and to prepare the crews completed a week's low level flying training but nothing could prepare them for the shock they would receive at the briefing when their target was announced.

The mission lived up to their fears. Of the 12 Lancasters that took part only five returned.

Augsburg was also one of the first operations where a new electronic navigation aid was used. Gee was a revolutionary system that used radio waves to plot an aircraft's course on a screen, a huge advance over the previous navigation systems based on a compass and the stars.

Harris believed that the quickest way to destroy Germany's war effort was to hit it with as many bombers as possible. On the night of 26 May 1942 over 1,000 bombers, virtually every serviceable training and front line aircraft in Bomber Command, dropped nearly 1,500 tons of bombs on the industrial facilities round Cologne. The damage was enormous and widespread and compared to previous raids a great success. However flying in pitch black meant that identifying targets for such large formations was a problem. The answer was the Pathfinder force. Formed in August 1942 their role was to locate and mark targets by dropping colour flares. The introduction of the Mosquito bomber gave the Pathfinders the perfect aircraft they needed for the job.

Using a new radar system called Oboe they were able to fly in advance and high above the bomber formations, mark the targets and get away at high speed.

By early February 1943 Bomber Command had been given new orders, **"The progressive destruction and dislocation of the German military, industrial and economic system and the undermining of the morale of the German people to the point where their capacity for armed resistance is fatally weakened."**

For four months Germany's industrial might was attacked by day by the American 8th Air Force and at night by Bomber Command. During the battle of Hamburg, the largest port in Europe, a lethal cocktail of high explosives and incendiaries was used for the first time. Virtually the whole city was wiped out by a raging firestorm killing 40,000 citizens.

An Avro Lancaster of 103 Squadron, Bomber Command. The most developed bomber of the European war and seldom challenged as the best

It's 1943 and Mosquito crews are planning for another night trip to bomb Berlin

CHAPTER 22

THE DAMBUSTERS

Not all of Bomber Command's raids were undertaken by hundreds of aircraft. In May 1943 19 Lancasters from a single squadron, 617, attacked the great dams of western Germany which provided the industrial heartland of Germany's Ruhr valley with much of its power. Led by the 24 year old Wing Commander Guy Gibson the squadron attacked the dams at very low level using unique bouncing bombs developed specially for the raid by Barnes Wallis. Two major dams were breached and, despite the loss of eight Lancasters, the raid proved that Bomber Command could deliver precision attacks successfully.

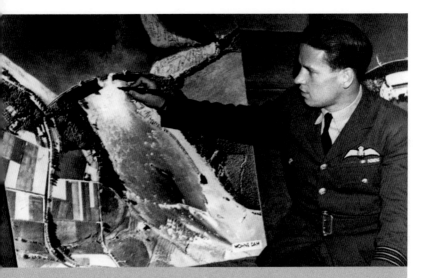

Wing Commander Guy Gibson, CO of 617 Squadron, with an aerial photograph showing the breached Mohne Dam

Vickers scientist and engineer Barnes Wallis who came up with the notion of a bouncing bomb to breach the dams

The underside of Guy Gibson's dams raid aircraft, AJ-G, showing the cylinder design of the bouncing bomb

Guy Gibson and his crew prepare for the dams raid. Gibson is at the top of the steps

CHAPTER 23

ROUND-THE-CLOCK

The last of the major targets for 1943 was the great prize Berlin. But here the campaign stumbled. From December to March 600 aircraft were lost to the strong defences, almost all Lancasters. Throughout that year Bomber Command lost 3,000 aircraft and 20,000 aircrew.

In June 1944 the allies landed in Normandy.

Bomber Command provided much needed support for ground forces as

An Avro Lancaster III of 635 Squadron marking the squadron's 100th operation of the war. They went to Chemnitz on 14 February 1945

Another shot of 103 Squadron Lancaster EE182, this time over Germany and being flown by Nicky Ross who would later volunteer for 617 Squadron

and when they met stiff opposition. At Caen the advance faltered so Bomber Command mounted a relentless attack that decimated the city.

After Normandy Bomber Command resumed the offensive with Germany's oil industry in its sights. By now round-the-clock raids had been firmly established in tandem with the

USAAF. What little opposition there was from the Luftwaffe was dealt with by long range escort fighters such as the Mustang, the first with the range to accompany the bombers all the way into the heart of Germany and back.

The bombing campaign had unleashed its awesome potential to cause destruction on a massive scale. Fac-

A heavily damaged Boeing B-17 of the US 8th Air Force caught in the middle of another aircraft's bomb drop. The B-17s suffered heavily on their daylight raids

tories had to be buried into mountains, railways and lines of communication were blown apart, thousands of anti aircraft guns and crews were kept from being deployed to the front line. The bombers could strike with impunity and total air supremacy. The Luftwaffe had run out of fuel. But Germany was still capable of fighting back. V1 flying bombs followed by V2 rockets had begun landing on Britain after the Normandy landings. No-one could tell where they would land and they were almost impossible to shoot down. Bomber Command had to do something so they successfully bombed the main rocket factories at Peenemunde on the Baltic coast.

By now the politicians were questioning the morality of such destruction. They began distancing themselves

The second nuclear bomb explosion in anger. This time over Nagasaki

A German V.2 rocket, the world's first long range guided missile. Over 3,000 of them were fired in the last eight months of the war causing death and destruction across Europe

from the bombing campaign. A totally devastated Germany was thought not to be in the best interests of the new Europe that would emerge from the rubble. Although they had played a major role the bombers had failed to force a German surrender. Then on 6 August 1945 a single American atomic bomb was dropped on Hiroshima. Armed with new atomic weapons the power of the bomber would never again be in doubt.

CHAPTER 24

COASTAL COMMAND AT WAR

At the outbreak of war Coastal Command had only 19 squadrons. Some were receiving new Sunderlands and Hudsons but most were equipped with ageing Avro Ansons that were soon to be taken out of front line duties.

Coastal Command had to be reinforced with aircraft from other commands. Bomber Command supplied Wellingtons and a few Hampdens in the early months of the war. Then a whole range of RAF bombers were diverted from their main role to carry out attacks on ships.

Probably the best known of the stop-gap aircraft was the Bristol Blenheim. In February 1940 Blenheim IV fighters were transferred from Fighter Command to help with convoy and fishing fleet protection. They were followed by Blenheim bombers used for daylight raids on channel shipping. They pressed home their attacks at mast

A formation of Blenheim Mk.IVs supplied to Coastal Command early in the war

A mainstay of Coastal during and after the war, the mammoth Short Sunderland carried bombs, mines and depth charges on anti-submarine patrols

height braving the flak to drop their bombs almost horizontally.

The bravery of the Blenheim crews cannot be underrated. They never faltered in their duties however difficult the target but unescorted as they usually were they often fell prey to marauding German fighters. At zero feet they had no room to manoeuvre and they hadn't the speed to get away.

CE Turner's great painting of a Coastal Command Lockheed Hudson bombing enemy shipping

CHAPTER 25

PROTECTING THE CONVOYS

Britain had always relied heavily on the sea lanes to bring supplies from all over the world. Now, isolated from Europe, she was almost entirely dependent on the convoys coming from America. If these routes weren't kept open the Second World War would inevitably be lost.

Throughout the war convoys from and to the USA, Russia, Canada and from other far-flung outposts in the Empire had to be defended from enemy attack. Germany attacked the convoys from above and below. Coastal Command, working closely with the navy, was at the centre of the struggle.

From the very first day of the war German U-boats and surface raiders prowled the Atlantic sinking merchant ships and strangling Britain's lifeline

A German U-boat, one of many responsible for sinking millions of tons of allied shipping during the war and therefore enemy number one for RAF Coastal Command

to the outside world. In the first three weeks alone almost 150,000 tons of shipping were sunk yet Coastal Command had no effective weapon to counter the problem. Standing patrols kept watch on German ports and when a U-boat was sighted Bomber Command would send aircraft to attack. Invariably they were too late. The problem grew more acute after June 1940 when the German capture of French Channel ports gave them a much shorter route to the South Atlantic.

The Sunderland was the one aircraft with the range to patrol more than 500 miles from shore. It could carry 2,000lbs

A painting showing a Sunderland escorting a vital supply convoy through the straits of Gibraltar

of bombs and bristled with so many machine guns that the Germans called it "the flying porcupine". But there were never enough Sunderlands to cover the vast expanse of the Atlantic.

In March 1941 the Sunderlands were joined by an American-built flying boat, the Consolidated Catalina. The Catalina had earned a reputation in the US Navy for rugged reliability and impressive endurance. Together the Sunderlands and Catalinas patrolled a

A Coastal Command Catalina flying protection over a Royal Navy minelayer off Britain's west coast on 14 July 1943

tion. Another aircraft from the Consolidated Corporation, built as a heavy bomber, the Liberator entered service with the RAF in June 1941 and immediately revolutionised Britain's defensive patrols. Flying mainly from bases in Northern Ireland Liberators could range 2,000 miles from British shores massively extending convoy protection.

However it was not until 1943 that specialist radar and better bombs reached the squadrons in sufficient quantity to improve their chances.

Until this time the Sunderlands had been effective only in denying the U-boats time enough on the surface to aim their torpedoes at their intended victim. Now, better equipped, they actually began to sink U-boats.

wide area from the frozen North Atlantic areas around Iceland to the warmer waters of the West African coast.

However the expanse of the Atlantic Ocean meant there was a gap beyond the range of Coastal Command aircraft. It became a rich hunting ground for U-boats. An even more powerful aircraft was required to bridge the gap.

The Liberator was the perfect solu-

One way to bridge the Atlantic gap, a RAF Consolidated Liberator brought from the USA to bolster escort and anti-submarine duties in mid-Atlantic

CHAPTER 26

SHIPPING STRIKE

As 1943 was a turning point for the struggle against the U-boats so it was for the war waged by the strike aircraft against enemy shipping. Many of the early attacks in the Channel and the North Sea had been carried out by torpedo-carrying Bristol Beauforts and the American Hudsons. Both aircraft had some success but because of its lack of speed and manoeuvrability

A Bristol Beaufort of 86 Squadron Coastal Command on an anti-shipping strike in 1941

the Beaufort, in particular, had suffered unacceptable losses. The Beaufighter, from the same stable was now used to solve Coastal Command's strike problem. Armed with a lethal cocktail of rockets, torpedoes and cannon, the Beaufighter revealed what a fast, heavily-armed aircraft could do against even well defended enemy convoys.

The arrival of Mosquitos in the strike wings was more good news. These versatile aircraft had already proved their effectiveness in the other commands and now added their power and speed to anti-shipping sorties.

Coastal Command was to play a pivotal role in the allied invasion of Europe. By the summer of 1944 the

command had grown to 71 squadrons ready to protect the massive invasion fleet gathering at ports all over the south of England. D-Day was imminent.

After the Normandy landings U-boats tried to get in among the fleet but were generally weeded out by the big patrol boats. In July 1944 alone Beaufighters made 500 separate attacks, sinking 22 German ships, ten of them in a single convoy. The German navy was virtually imprisoned in their ports.

The invasion had deprived the few remaining U-boats of their French ports and the Coastal Command strike wings held sway over all surface shipping.

A Bristol Beaufighter firing rockets at enemy shipping

A Beaufighter of 236 Squadron as part of the North Coates Strike Wing in 1943

A De Havilland Mosquito Mk.XVIII, nicknamed 'Tsetse' because of its sting and photographed in November 1943. The aircraft was fitted with a Molins 6pdr cannon and could fire huge projectiles at enemy shipping

CHAPTER 27

RESCUE AT SEA

Throughout the war perhaps the single biggest problem for the RAF was the loss of experienced aircrew. However every effort was made to save those shot down over the sea. The success rate was already one in three but better organisation could improve even this figure. In June 1941 control of air sea rescue services was handed to Coastal Command.

Crews flying the Supermarine Walrus were responsible for saving thousands of lives and rescuing downed pilots and crew from the sea

Over 10,000 people were picked up by the rescue squadrons during the war and every single such rescue bolstered the morale of all those involved.

One of the most famous rescue aircraft was the little Supermarine Walrus amphibian or 'shagbat' as it was affectionately known. Designed as a catapult aircraft for use on battleships it entered service in 1936. Its new life in Coastal Command air-sea rescue squadrons started five years later.

Later the Walrus was replaced by the Sea Otter, a longer range version, the last biplane ever to see service with the RAF.

The Supermarine Sea Otter followed the Walrus into service becoming the RAF's final ever biplane

CHAPTER 28

TRANSPORT COMMAND AT WAR

Perhaps the most significant development in air transport in the 1930s was the parachute. Parachuting had been a popular sport across Europe since the early years of peace and parachute drops were a regular feature of the inter-war air displays.

However it was the Russians who first saw its military potential. As early as the 1920s they demonstrated a number of unorthodox methods for deploying troops from aircraft including climbing out onto the wing and sliding off the back! These demonstrations were performed in front of officers from America and Britain who concluded airborne deployment of troops had no use in modern warfare. But, to the watching Germans the parachute aroused extreme interest.

The Luftwaffe's Junkers Ju52 was used before the war for parachute training as well as troop carrying and supply delivery

Armstrong Whitworth Whitleys were used for practice parachute dropping from 1940

They began to use their Junkers Ju-52 airliner as a transport aircraft during secret, illicit, paratroop training in Russia. This training was to pay off when German paratroops and gliders spearheaded the Blitzkrieg that hit the Low Countries and France, in May 1940.

In 1940 Winston Churchill called for the formation of a force of about 5,000 parachute and gliderborne troops to be used for quick in and out raids into continental Europe. He called them 'butcher and bolt' raids.

Number 70 Group, RAF was formed to provide the training aircraft. It was based at Ringway, now the site of Manchester airport.

Not for the first time, internal rivalry hindered development of a new idea.

The RAF had no such thing as a purpose-built paratroop aircraft and Bomber Command who at that time, provided the only means of attacking Germany, were reluctant to give up any of their precious bombers. In the end, a few ageing Whitleys were supplied.

The other means of delivering troops by air was in gliders which provided a comparatively cheap form of transport and did not impose on the aircraft manufacturers' ability to maintain production of warplanes. Since their role was to deliver shock troops, they had the advantages of being silent and able to land on sites inaccessible to powered aircraft.

Although glider pilots came from the army, they were trained by the RAF. Not surprisingly a glider pilot's job was extremely dangerous and the high number of fatalities meant that RAF pilots were increasingly needed to do the job

The first operations using airborne troops were successful enough to persuade the government to enlarge the force and make it available for more ambitious missions. 38 Wing RAF was set up in 1943 to provide all transportation needs.

This was part of a new Transport Command which had been given responsibility across all theatres of war.

One of its most critical roles was ferrying replacement aircraft from factories and safe havens well out of the reach of Germany and her allies. Crews had to be trained to use a wide range of aircraft. Pilots then had to deliver aircraft to airfields all over the world. Many pilots flew every type operated by the RAF as well as being the first to fly new aircraft coming from America.

Terence Cuneo's action packed wartime painting of Horsa gliders spewing out men and machinery on D-Day

CHAPTER 29

ENTER THE DAKOTA

One of the most famous American aircraft was the Douglas Dakota which would become the most celebrated of all transport aircraft, staying in service with the RAF for almost 30 years. The Dakota proved perfect for the role and was the only allied aircraft used for the main paratroop drops of the war. One of its many advantages was an ability to fly at 110 mph a speed at which paratroopers would not be hit by the slipstream.

The Dakota carried up to 18 fully-laden men or three tons of equipment

The ubiquitous American Douglas C-47 used by British forces as the Dakota

British paratroops fitting harnesses before entering a Dakota. This was a large scale exercise on 22 April 1944 as training for D-Day drops

The Douglas Dakota III operated by the Battle of Britain Memorial Flight and wearing D-Day identification stripes (15.08.2014)

and could land on short, makeshift airstrips. The means of delivering special forces, crucial to the success of an invasion, was now in place.

D-Day minus one, 5 June 1944. Pathfinder troops clambered into flimsy gliders and Dakotas to form the vanguard of the forces that would liberate Europe.

By 6 June RAF transports mounted round-the-clock missions ferrying supplies and equipment to reinforce the allied positions. As the allies broke out across Normandy into occupied Europe, the aircraft of Transport Command were to be crucial in maintaining their offensive.

But not all airborne missions were to prove successful. At Arnhem in Holland, nearly 8.000 soldiers of 1st Airborne Division were cut off from supplies and reinforcements. Despite desperate efforts by Transport Command to relieve them bad weather and strong German defences prevented them from always getting through.

The failure of the operation meant that an opportunity to end the war quickly had been lost. But the lessons that were learned were to be put to good use within a few months.

CHAPTER 30

LANDING BY MOONLIGHT

Part of the success of the liberating armies in France was due to the clandestine activities of Resistance fighters controlled by agents of the Special Operations Executive. These men and women were flown into occupied territories under the cover of darkness, landing in remote fields.

The Westland Lysander was designed as an army co-operation aircraft but it made its name in special duties squadrons flying these cloak and dagger missions.

The Lysander was ideal for the role. Fitted with extra fuel tanks, it could reach far into the South of France. Its low landing speed meant it could put down in a small field and its high wing design gave the pilot a wonderful field of vision when looking for the torches which the French Resistance workers used to mark the landing strip.

These were hazardous long-range flights, at night, to deliver and pick-up agents or VIPs but they were keeping open a vital line of communication be-

A Westland Lysander operated by 161 (Special Duties) Squadron. These specially converted aircraft included extra fuel and oil tanks, a rear bench seat and a fixed ladder

Westland Lysanders of 4 (AC) Squadron which were used for general reconnaissance and coastal patrols early in the war

tween Britain and the French resistance movement.

There is no doubt that these pilots, and the men and women they trans-ported, played an important part in the war. Through them, French resistance was kept supplied with information, weapons and stores.

161 Squadron pilots including the famous Hugh Verity (second from left), author of We Landed By Moonlight, his story of flying SOE operations into occupied France

CHAPTER 31

OPERATION VARSITY

In contrast to these single aircraft missions, the allies were planning what was to be the largest and last airborne operation of the war - the Rhine Crossing.

The Rhine was the last natural barrier the allies faced on the way to the heart of Germany. On 24 March 1945 pilots of Transport Command helped to carry over 21,000 paratroopers and infantry across the Rhine in an extraordinary show of strength.

Within hours the allies had secured a foothold and were advancing through Germany.

Sweeping through Germany the allies linked up with the Russian forces advancing from the East. The Reich buckled under the strain and by May the war was over.

Handley Page Halifax ready to tow a Horsa glider across the Rhine

Those that didn't get across by air spent dangerous minutes crossing the Rhine by other means

CHAPTER 32

WAR IN THE FAR EAST

The war had started badly for the RAF. They were undermanned and with many inexperienced crews but the biggest problem was the lack of both quantity and quality of aircraft.

To make matters worse the quality and performance of the Japanese aircraft astonished British commanders with the Zero, in particular, being shown to be a top class fighter.

The biggest issues for the allied forces were the enormous distances both for delivering replacement aircraft and in theatre itself. From Northern India to Singapore, for example, it is almost 2,000 miles, a huge area to cover, much of it over impenetrable jungle. Without diminishing the vital work of the fighters and bombers perhaps the single most important aspect of the war was the work of the transport crews resupplying the troops on the front line.

Imphal is near the India-Burma border and bore the brunt, along with Kohima, of the Japanese advance during the Spring of 1944. While the Hurribombers from the fighter squadrons maintained a constant assault on Japanese positions, the men on the ground were completely reliant on the transports to provide supplies. The Dakotas dropped hundreds of tons a day in terrible weather conditions. As the Japanese retreated the problems just increased. Now the supply lines got longer and the crews flew their Dakotas over huge areas of impenetrable jungle in search of their drop or landing zones. In the first four months of 1945 210,000 tons of supplies arrived by air, that's almost five times the amount received from all other methods, a testament to the importance of air supply.

67 Squadron Brewster Buffalos being assembled in Singapore in 1941. The Buffalo was considered good enough for air defence in Asia but failed against superior Japanese fighters

RAF Dakota loads up with troops from West Africa to take them deep into the heart of Burma

RAF Dakota loadmasters prepare to drop supplies to the Chindits in the Burmese jungle

CHAPTER 33

FIGHTER COMMAND IN THE COLD WAR

By the end of the war in 1945 the Luftwaffe had been utterly defeated. However for a year before they had possession of an aircraft capable of changing the course of the conflict, the Messerschmitt Me262, Germany's first operational jet aircraft. It was heavily-armed and with a top speed well in excess of 500mph. But even then jet propulsion was not a new concept.

Frank, later Sir Frank, Whittle, a pilot officer in the RAF, developed the world's first jet engine in 1930 but it would be another 11 years before a British aircraft would fly using his concept. When jet development finally got under way in Britain the Whittle engine was tested in a Gloster-built airframe and it was a Gloster aircraft, the Meteor, that became the RAF's first jet fighter. Two Rolls Royce engines, each delivering 1,700lbs of thrust, gave the Meteor a speed of around 400mph and a rate of climb of over 2,000 feet per min. This performance would be greatly improved in later marks but

The world's first operational jet fighter the Messerschmitt Me262

Gloster Meteor, Britain's first jet fighter, used by De Havilland to test the Goblin engine in 1945

the Meteor's armament remained a traditional fighter configuration of four 20mm cannon. Most Meteors operating in Europe were used against the V1 flying bombs but jet aircraft played very little part in the war itself and had no effect on its outcome. However the Me262 and the Meteor set the standard for postwar military aircraft.

The main role of Fighter Command had always been home defence and by the time of the Coronation Review in 1953 Britain had the largest air force in Europe. Security was once again at the top of the agenda. The West's relations with the Soviet Union had deteriorated rapidly after the war culminating in the closure of all land routes into Berlin and the explosion of the first Soviet nuclear bomb. Although the Soviet aircraft industry had lagged behind that of their former allies now they were rapidly developing aircraft to compete with the best in the world.

In 1947 the British government had sanctioned the export of a number of

The sleek and beautiful Hawker Hunter. This aircraft, WB188, was the prototype and broke the world air speed record by flying at 727mph in 1953 with test pilot Neville Duke at the controls

A Canadair CL-13 Sabre F.4 of 234 Squadron at RAF Oldenburg in Germany late in 1953

Rolls Royce jet engines which became the power plant for the latest and most impressive Soviet fighter, the Mig 15.

This aircraft first saw active service in 1950 during the Korean War and was immediately successful. Meteors flown by the RAAF were no match for the Migs. The revelation of the Meteor as virtually obsolete was a nasty shock for the RAF. More so because the post-war budget had also cut research funding which meant that no natural successor was anywhere near completion. To fill the gap swept-wing Sabres, which had been so successful in Korea, were bought from America. This aircraft pushed the limits of fighter performance to a new level with a top speed of just below the speed of sound. The Sabres started to arrive in Germany in 1952 equipping front line squadrons with an aircraft that could counter the Soviet Migs. They would stay for four years until the new British jet fighters were ready.

The first new aircraft to arrive were out of the stable that had given the RAF the Spitfire and the Hurricane. They were the Supermarine Swift and the Hawker Hunter. The Swift proved to be unsatisfactory but the Hunter was a versatile combat aircraft and became the backbone of Fighter Command. It was a pilot's dream. It represented a new step forward in performance being capable of over 700mph and achieved a service ceiling of over 51,000 feet. Easy to fly, responsive to pilots' needs and capable of taking on many roles the Hunter also proved to be a winner in the export market.

The Hunter could carry a wide range of weaponry including the powerful 30mm Aden cannon as well as bombs for ground attack. Hunters flew with squadrons in Germany and the UK as well as taking an active role in the Suez crisis, in Kuwait and in Borneo.

The Black Arrows formation team

flew Hunters and showed off the aircraft's extraordinary aerobatic abilities to the world. They created a sensation at the Farnborough Airshow in 1958 by flying a formation loop with no less than 22 aircraft.

The Gloster Javelin was the first delta-wing aircraft in the RAF and was designed as a two-seat all-weather interceptor. It came on the scene in 1956 but its performance was disappointingly inferior compared to the Hunter, However its ability to carry extra radar did make it suitable for night fighting.

By the mid 50s the Mig 21, a supersonic aircraft, had entered service with the Soviet Air Force. Once again the performance ante had been increased. Furthermore the Soviets now had a powerful force of jet-powered nuclear bombers and, with weapons of mass destruction, it only needed just one bomber to get through.

Skilled hands are needed to keep the aircraft flying

EX-AIRMEN .. JOIN THE

RAF

UNDER THE SHORT TERM **£125** BOUNTY SCHEME

An RAF recruitment poster trying to persuade ex airmen to rejoin the force after the war

A Gloster Javelin FAW8 of 41 Squadron in 1960

CHAPTER 34

THE RAF GOES SUPERSONIC

The 1957 Defence White Paper proposed that a new generation of jet bombers, the V-force, should carry Britain's nuclear deterrent. This force was to be supplemented by ground-launched ballistic missiles. The main task of the fighters would be to defend the bomber bases from attack. In the immediate future fighters would be equipped with air-to-air missiles but in the long term the plan was that surface-to-air missiles would replace fighters altogether. It looked like the dogfighter had its day.

Five Lightnings of 56 Squadron flying in formation

However one aircraft project was already so advanced and the level of increased performance so dramatic that its progress was not interrupted. The result was the English Electric Lightning, the first and only completely British supersonic interceptor ever to fly with the RAF.

It embraced the American concept of a completely integrated weapons platform with all aspects of engines, armament, airframe and radar de-

Roland Beamont was English Electric's chief test pilot flying the Canberra, Lightning and TSR2 in an illustrious post-war career

veloped together to create the perfect fighter aircraft. With a maximum speed of Mach 2.3 or 1500mph, a ceiling of 60,000ft and a rapid rate of climb the Lightning outperformed every other aircraft in the RAF.

It also added a new dimension to air defence, air-to-air missiles. Although twin 30mm cannon for engaging enemy fighters were added in later marks the Lightning was not really a dogfighter at all however it was such an advance on previous interceptors that it was able to carry out the fighter role

for the next ten years. It also brought back confidence to the pilots. As one said *"we know that we can catch any current bomber and we know we can outfight any fighter. This knowledge that we have the finest interceptor in the world gives the pilots tremendous confidence."*

Advances in radar technology lead to the opening of a new early warning system which could look far over the horizon. Combining this ground based radar system with the Lightning meant that for the foreseeable future manned

Squadron Leader John Howe, CO of 74 Squadron in 1960 when they became the first squadron to equip with the Lightning F.1

aircraft still had a significant role.

From 1961 Fighter Command was assigned to Supreme Allied Commander Europe with a specific responsibility for aerial approaches to Great Britain and the defence of the strategic bomber force. The sight of pilots near their aircraft on instant readiness waiting for the radar web to show up an enemy echoed the days of 1940.

Organisational changes in 1964 were followed by the cancellation of a number of advanced aircraft projects. The Lightning would have to stay in service for many years as Britain's front-line interceptor.

However by the late 1960s ground-to-air missiles, the latest radar and the use of supersonic interceptors made high altitude bombers extremely vulnerable. In response both the Soviets and NATO developed aircraft that could fly effectively at much lower levels making them invisible to radar. The newly formed RAF Strike Command now needed a radar that would look down on the enemy. Ageing Shackletons were hastily converted to provide an advanced early warning system. They were supplemented by the purchase of McDonnell Douglas Phantoms from America which were the first fighters flown by the RAF with an ability to look down on low flying targets.

The supersonic Phantom had been battle-proven in the Vietnam War and was capable of carrying an impressive array of bombs, rockets and cannon. Phantom pilots had discovered that the aircraft had the ability to perform a task that by now should have been obsolete. In Vietnam Migs proved able to turn inside rockets launched at them by the Phantoms and fly back and engage the now defenceless aircraft . Armaments for short range protection and the pilot skills to manoeuvre the aircraft were a necessity. Dogfighting was back.

The ambitious and highly-advanced BAC TSR2 was eagerly awaited by the RAF but cancelled by the Labour government in 1965

An RAF McDonnell Douglas Phanton RF-4 in flight in 1980

CHAPTER 35

BOMBER COMMAND IN THE COLD WAR

By 1948 Bomber Command's strength in Britain was cut from 97 squadrons to 24. They were flying ageing Mosquitoes, Lancasters and Lincolns. Western relations with Soviet Russia were deteriorating and the newly formed North Atlantic Treaty Organisation, NATO, was standing by for Soviet aggression. The news of the detonating of a Soviet atomic bomb reverberated round the world. Soon afterwards, with Russian support, the North Koreans invaded South Korea. The world was at the brink of another war so a massive western rearmament programme began.

The war was over but there was a new enemy. The Berlin Wall was just another sign that relations with the Soviet Union were decaying rapidly

Avro Lincolns of 83 Squadron. The Lincoln was the last piston-engined bomber in the RAF and was soon replaced by the first of the jet bombers

CHAPTER 36

THE V-FORCE

With no aircraft capable of delivering an atomic bomb the RAF bought Boeing B-29s from America. Renamed the Washington the B-29 did not impress the RAF. However they lasted barely two years as Bomber Command had just entered the jet age with the arrival of the new English Electric Canberra on front line duty. Although it was popular with air crews senior officers were disappointed that they didn't have the heavy jet bomber they now needed. Although it was subsonic the Canberra allowed the RAF to deploy a jet bomber to Germany where it would be nearest to the forces of the Warsaw Pact. It was to undertake high level reconnaissance missions as part of its NATO obligations for many years.

Canberra B.2s of 12 Squadron. This amazing aircraft took its frontline place in Bomber Command in 1951 but was still providing vital service in other roles more than 50 years later

But it was the V bomber force that put the RAF firmly back on the world map.

The Boeing B.29 Washington was bought for the RAF but left little impression with RAF commanders

The crew of this Vickers Valiant, XD822, took part in Operation Grapple, the testing of Britain's first Hydrogen bomb from Christmas Island in May 1957

The first production Vulcan B Mk.1, XA889, on display at Farnborough in 1957, the year the Vulcan went into service with the RAF

Union and back. They had to fly high, 50,000 feet, way beyond the reach of Soviet ground defences. And they had to be fast enough to outrun enemy fighters.

The first of the V bombers, the Vickers Valiant, entered service in 1955. Within two years four squadrons had been equipped. Deployed in the Suez crisis in 1956 Valiants dropped conventional bombs on Egyptian air-fields but the V Force was dealt a massive blow when fatigue problems were found in the Valiants. The damage was too expensive to repair and within two months they were scrapped.

The real power of the V Force was revealed with the arrival of the Avro Vulcan and the Handley Page Victor.

The delta-wing Vulcan was one of the most awesome aircraft ever to serve with the RAF. The B Mk.1 entered service in 1957 but the uprated B.2 was by far the most effective weapon in Britain's nuclear arsenal. The Vulcan had a range of over 3,000 miles, a top speed of close to the speed of sound and a service ceiling of 55,000 feet. The Vulcan was an outstanding aircraft.

It carried Britain's nuclear deterrent and formed the basis of the country's entire defence policy for 12 years.

The requirements for atomic bomb carriers were very exacting. They had to be able to get to the heart of the Soviet

The graceful crescent wing Victor was the last V bomber to enter service and the most adaptable. It had an enormous bay which could carry up to 40,000 lbs of bombs. The Victor would remain in service for many years and was indispensable as a tanker for air-to-air refuelling other aircraft well into the 1990s. However the Soviet Union now had the capability to launch pre-emptive strikes against the West. Airfields were likely to be among the first targets hit so the V bombers were dispersed to different airfields in the belief that in the event of an attack at least some of them would get airborne and, because nuclear war would probably come without notice, the Quick Reaction Alert was developed.

The aircraft were modified so that all the electronic systems for the four engines could be powered up from a single button. With practice the V bombers could be airborne in four minutes on their way to Moscow.

The V Force had to carry their nuclear weapons all the way to the target but the Soviet defences would be tough to penetrate so thoughts turned to bombs that could be released hundreds of miles away and then fly on to their targets. American Skybolt missiles fitted with British nuclear warheads seemed to be the solution. The V Force would be able to launch them on Moscow from up to a thousand miles away. But then the Americans cancelled the Skybolt project so the RAF bought Blue Steel missiles from Avro instead. Although it was British-made Blue Steel was second choice to Skybolt as the aircraft had to be 800 miles closer to their target before the weapons could be released.

Before Blue Steel became operational a Russian missile shot down an American U2 spyplane flying high over the Soviet Union. This single event radically altered V Force tactics. Vulcans and Victors had an operational

Underrated but hugely impressive, the Buccaneer was an ex-Royal Navy low-level nuclear bomber that played a vital role in the RAF for more than 20 years. This S.2 is XV333 from 208 Squadron.

altitude of 50,000 feet but the U2 was shot down at 60,000 feet. Altitude was no longer a defence. After years and years of reaching for the stars bombers of the V Force had to relearn hedge hopping and low level bombing so shaping aircraft design for the future.

TSR2 was expected to be a low and medium level nuclear or conventional bomber with reconnaissance capabilities. It would be fast but with STOL capabilities and operate in all weathers, day or night.

Throughout the Sixties the V Force played a major role in the defence of Britain and Western Europe but no-one was ever sure if, when the time came, the bombers could penetrate Soviet defences. It looked as though the manned nuclear bomber had its day. Ground launched ballistic missiles now became the nuclear weapon of choice. The V bombers carried on until 1969 but finally, with the introduction of the first British nuclear submarines armed with Polaris missiles, the role of strategic deterrence passed back to the Royal Navy.

This wasn't quite the end of the V Force altogether as a series of high

Polaris, Britain's new submarine-launched weapon, took the nuclear responsibility from the RAF in 1969

profile aircraft project cancellations forced the RAF to extend the life of these aircraft. The most far-reaching of these cancellations was that of the TSR2. Designed as a replacement for Canberra it was built by BAC, an uneasy alliance formed by the merger of English Electric, Vickers and Bristol Aircraft. TSR2 was an advanced project which first flew in 1964. However it was such a complex aircraft to manufacture that costs soared. The government, under pressure to reduce debts, cancelled the project. This was a major blow to the RAF.

Huge development costs had already forced the government to delay or cancel other projects and now its principal strike aircraft had been shot down in flames.

The government now placed orders for the F.111 and then cancelled that too. Fortunately the navy was reducing the size of their carrier fleet and so their Buccaneer aircraft were transferred to the RAF. Ironically the RAF had rejected Buccaneer some years previously as they had been expecting TSR2. The Buccaneer turned out to be ideally cast in the ultra low level strike role. It flew under the radar hugging the ground and withstanding the tremendous buffeting at heights of less than 200 feet. It also had a very long life, still in service during the Gulf War of 1991, 22 years after it had first entered service. The Buccaneer was the RAF's last purpose-built bomber.

When the US cancelled Skybolt Britain turned to a home-grown alternative, Avro's Blue Steel, seen here being taken towards a 617 Squadron Vulcan

In 1968 Bomber Command was merged with Fighter Command to form Strike Command. The future of Britain's strike force now lay with multi-role aircraft like the Tornado, designed to satisfy the needs of many nations who also helped bear the immense development costs.

The Handley Page Victor was the last of the V-bombers and spent many years as a tanker. Here is a Victor K Mk.2

CHAPTER 37

THE COMING OF THE HELICOPTER

Perhaps the most radical development for the RAF was the arrival in Transport Command, and later in Coastal Command, of the helicopter. The remaining amphibians continued to work together with marine launches until the first air sea rescue helicopters arrived in the mid 1950s.

The ability of helicopters to hover literally added a new dimension to rescue activities and despite their principal service role the all yellow Westland Whirlwinds and Wessex became a familiar sight res-

Cpl Brian Robinson looks over a disused Japanese wartime airstrip from his Westland Whirlwing HAR10 in Labuan Island, Borneo in 1960

The easily identifiable yellow search and rescue Westland Wessex HC2 which served with the RAF from 1964

cuing civilians from the sea, cliff faces and other inaccessible places.

The helicopter proved its value in the jungles of Malaya in the 1950's where it demonstrated its unique ability to get in and out of the most confined spaces to evacuate casualties or drop off supplies.

But, as late as 1960, the RAF still lacked a helicopter capable of lifting battlefield equipment. The introduction of the Belvedere in 1961 went some way to improve the situation. But in 1969, after a series of disastrous crashes, the Belvedere was withdrawn.

For 10 years the RAF considered a replacement but always gave a higher priority to fixed-wing aircraft. It was not until 1980 that the first of 41 Boeing Chinooks entered service. These twin-engined monsters lift up to 25,000 lbs, five times more than the Belvedere could manage. Their use greatly reinforces RAF's capability in battlefield support.

RAF Whirlwind of 110 Squadron providing air support for the army at Nanga Gaat in Borneo in 1963

A 66 Squadron Bristol Belvedere heavylift helicopter based at Seletar in Singapore in the 1960s

An RAF Chinook flying over Afghanistan on 25 March 2015. The Chinook crews have been responsible for evacuating 13,000 casualties during the campaign and many of them have received decorations (25.03.2015)

CHAPTER 38

COASTAL COMMAND IN THE COLD WAR

The post-war period brought new challenges for Coastal Command and, in line with the rest of the RAF, substantial cuts reduced the force to a shadow of its former self. The long-range Liberators and Catalinas were returned to America leaving a glaring gap in anti-submarine capabilities.

By 1950 it was obvious that the Soviet Union was rearming at an alarming pace and the Berlin blockade had proved once again that they were prepared to back their Communist ideals with force. Known Soviet expansion plans included the building of a substantial surface and submarine fleet. For this reason, therefore, the role of RAF Coastal Command was at the top of the defence agenda.

During the setting up of NATO it was agreed that Britain's responsibilities would include the provision of more forces in the eastern Atlantic. Inevitably this meant more aircraft and arrangements were made to bring in a number of Lockheed Neptune medi-

The Lockheed Neptune proved to be a worthy addition to Britain's maritime force during the mid 1950s

The Short Sunderland continued on into the 1950s and contributed more than 20 years service

A Shackleton MR3 of 201 Squadron on a maritime patrol. This aircraft, XF710, crashed in Scotland in 1964

In 1972 8 Squadron took delivery of 12 modified Shackletons, fitted with the AN/APS-20 radar to handle the airborne early warning role. This temporary measure lasted almost 20 more years

um-range maritime reconnaissance aircraft from the United States. What the Neptune lacked in performance was made up for by strong attack and search radar systems. It proved to be a worthy stop-gap aircraft until new British designs were available.

Throughout the post-war years the RAF was regularly called on to help out in a number of localised conflicts round the world. Two squadrons of Sunderlands played an important reconnaissance role during the Malayan emergency as part of a substantial RAF force. Communist guerillas, originally armed by the British during the war, were now supported by a large community of Chinese sympathisers in their struggle for independence. The emergency lasted until 1960 tying up scarce RAF resources that would have been welcome in the defence of Europe. The same squadrons of Sunderlands now became Britain's only contribution to the Korean conflict supporting the United Nations forces. They flew more than 1,000 missions helping to blockade North Korean ports.

By the 1950s the age of the flying boat was finally over. There has never been a better example of classic design and adaptability in the RAF than the Sunderland.

During the war Liberators had proved that long-range land planes could be as effective as flying boats for maritime patrol. The obvious replacement for the Sunderland was the Avro Shackleton.

When the Shackleton entered service in 1951 it had been in development for some years. Now new navigation and radar equipment had to be tested and then there was a long period of retraining for the crews. The aircraft passed all the tests with flying colours except one. One of the distinctive features of the Shackleton was the roar of its Rolls Royce Griffon engines. It was a sound that stirred the hearts of the British public bringing back memories of the Griffon-engined Spitfires of the late war years but that inspiring noise did little for the crews who had to spend up to

22 hours on each patrol listening to it which, some ineffective engine muffling apart, they did for the next 40 years.

The 1957 Defence White Paper made enormous cuts in the RAF as a whole but Coastal Command came out of it better than most.

With the added strike capability of a newly developed homing torpedo the Shackleton was an important part of NATO's plans. However the demise of the Sunderland and the planned phasing out of the Neptune would leave the Shackleton as the only fixed-wing aircraft in the command.

There were just ten squadrons of Shackletons to take on all the maritime responsibilities. They patrolled the Atlantic. They took part in combined exercises and three of the ten squadrons were tied up in the Mediterranean to counter the growing Soviet presence. One squadron even took on a bombing role dropping over 300 tons of bombs on Oman in 1958.

By 1969 each of these old piston-engined aircraft had flown thousands of hours and it was time to replace them with a more modern jet aircraft. The old command had also outlived its usefulness being merged into the recently formed Strike Command in 1969. It was replaced with the newly designated 18 Group. It seemed everything was going to change under the new system but the Shackleton wasn't going to be killed off that easily.

In the early Seventies the RAF was a slimmed down tight knit force.

Flexibility of response was the order of the day but there was one glaring gap in the RAF's arsenal. They had no airborne early warning aircraft to locate incoming intruders. The 1957 cuts had foreseen the demise of the aircraft carrier as a weapon of war. The carrier fleet was disbanded and their Fairey Gannett airborne early warning aircraft went with them. The planned early warning Nimrod had not yet taken off from the drawing board. In the interim the RAF turned again to the good old Shackleton.

Now these 20 year old aircraft were fitted with a forest of antennae and sported a new bulge under the nose to carry the radar. The old workhorse had learned new tricks and was carrying out one of the RAF's most important jobs. Their radar could spot potentially hostile intruders many miles away. They would vector air defence fighters to intercept and watch them carry it out on the screens. They found themselves working with the Phantoms brought in to bolster the strike capability. After five years what was intended to be a temporary arrangement until the Nimrod AEW was ready was still going strong.

In 1986 it was decided not to use Nimrods in this role at all. Instead an American aircraft, the Boeing E-3D Sentry, was ordered. Finally the Shackletons were scrapped. The 12 AEW variants had performed 38 years of service, 18 as maritime patrollers and 20 in their reincarnated role.

After £1 billion was spent and ten years of development the Nimrod AEW programme was cancelled in favour of the Boeing Sentry

An RAF Boeing E-3D Sentry from 23 Squadron based at RAF Waddington in Lincolnshire (24.09.2002)

CHAPTER 39

THE MIGHTY HUNTER

In fact the RAF had received its first maritime reconnaissance Nimrods in 1969. Developed from civilian De Havilland Comets the Nimrod reflected the very latest in technology and was the first four-jet maritime reconnaissance aircraft to enter service with any of the world's air forces.

These new aircraft gave the RAF a much improved range and endurance. At more than 1,000 miles away from its base the Nimrod could spend six hours on patrol in the danger area. From 1980 uprated Mk 2s began to arrive with the vastly superior EMI Searchwater long range radar, generally regarded as the finest system in the world.

It was the Falklands War in 1982 that turned the Nimrod into a powerful force. Sidewinder missiles were added for self-defence. They were followed by the destructive Harpoon anti-ship missile capable of being launched from a range of 75 miles.

For more than 40 years Nimrods patrolled the Iceland UK gap and the Western Approaches with consummate skill. Their surveillance capabilities ensured early warning of any Soviet ships or submarines and, after the Soviet threat diminished, the Nimrods were still employed in watching Britain's national waters defending the fishing fleets and the oil fields.

An RAF Nimrod MR2 takes off from Seeb airport in Oman for a patrol in the Gulf during the 2003 Iraq war

The RAF's first seven Nimrod MR1s delivered from October 1969

CHAPTER 40

TRANSPORT COMMAND IN THE COLD WAR

After the end of the war in 1945 most of the Dakotas were returned to the United States, but some were purchased for the RAF to use until new replacements could be produced.

The first of those was the Avro York, an assault transport, which entered service in 1943. The wartime use of Dakotas delayed the York development and it was 1948 before six squadrons were equipped. This was just in time for the massive airlift of food and other supplies to Berlin..

The Soviet Union had cut all the road and rail routes into Berlin from the British and American sectors of Germany effectively starving all Berliners not living in the Eastern, Communist Zone.

This action was the culmination of long arguments over the control of Germany after the war and gave the West a pointer to future Soviet hardline policy.

Within four days Transport Command and the US Air Force had joined forces to airlift supplies to the beleaguered citizens of West Berlin.

For more than 10 months aircraft

RAF Avro Yorks on the flight line at Wunsdorf during the Berlin Airlift

A Bristol Britannia C.1 of 511 Squadron RAF Transport Command takes off from Gatow in Germany in 1967

took off at the rate of one every three minutes, day and night, delivering thousands of tons of food, coal and equipment.

Dakotas and Yorks bore the brunt of the airlift, joined by Sunderlands of Coastal Command when their base on Lake Havel was not frozen over. The Soviets were amazed that the city could be supplied purely by air, even in the depths of winter, and eventually, when it was obvious that the blockade wasn't working they allowed road and rail communications across Germany to re-open.

The Berlin Airlift had stretched Transport Command to the limit. But the importance of resupply had been proven beyond doubt. Even so, the burning need to build up fighter and bomber strength still left transport at the bottom of the list of the government's defence priorities. And, by 1951, the magnificent effort of the

The Handley Page Hastings was the first new transport aircraft delivered post-war. Here TG582 delivers supplies to Christmas Island for the start of Operation Grapple in 1956

Berlin airlift just a memory, Transport Command had been whittled down to barely 50 aircraft.

In the 1950s Transport Command began to receive new aircraft as part of the RAF's overall expansion and modernisation plans.

The Handley Page Hastings had actually taken part in the last stages of the Berlin Airlift and was joined in 1956 by the Blackburn Beverley. The Beverley was considered to be an ugly monster by aircrew but quickly proved its worth.

A huge payload and impressive short take-off and landing abilities made it perfect for resupply in remote areas.

As Britain began withdrawing forces from around the world, transports which had previously been used for tactical resupply now took on strategic importance.

De Havilland Comet C.2s and C.4s of 216 Squadron ready to go at Lyneham in 1964

The RAF's heavy lift capability improved dramatically when the Blackburn Beverley entered service in 1957. 30 Squadron's XH124 is seen here at Bahrain in 1960

CHAPTER 41

AIR-TO-AIR REFUELLING

The closure of RAF bases around the world meant that Transport Command faced the prospect of having to fly further to their destinations without having the facility to re-fuel. The solution lay in the emerging ability of aircraft to re-fuel each other whilst in flight.

During the Cold War the RAF deployed standing patrols to watch for Soviet intruders. The jet fighters, in particular, had only short endurance and the ability to refuel in flight greatly extended their useful flying time and multiplied the effect of the force.

Refuelling systems were pioneered by Sir Alan Cobham, a First World War pilot, who had become a favourite on the air display circuit between the wars with his famous flying circus. In the early thirties Cobham made a number of long distance flights using a second aircraft with a weighted hose to deliver fuel to his Airspeed Courier.

Although leaning out of the aircraft with a steel hook to catch the hose seemed an impractical

method, he continued with his experiments.

The Air Ministry gave him little encouragement until the invention of the probe and drogue system.

In 1949 Flight Refuelling set up an endurance record in a Meteor jet fighter using a Lancaster as the tanker. In 12 hours and three minutes the Meteor was refuelled ten times. From the Fifties refuelling probes were fitted to all front-line aircraft and a growing fleet of tankers was created.

The Valiants were intended to be the main tanker aircraft, but fatigue ended

Flight Refuelling founder Sir Alan Cobham before an air-to-air test. The aircraft is Lancaster G-AHJT in 1947

Cobham used Handley Page Harrow G-AFRL for trials before the war

tive proposition.

The De Havilland Comet become the first commercial jet airliner when the series 1 joined BOAC in 1952. Transport Command chose this new type and series 2 Comets became the first jet military transports in 1956.

Comet was not the only passenger airliner to join the RAF. In 1959, military versions of the Bristol Britannia were enlisted. These turboprop aircraft had the longest range of all at over 5,000 miles.

These aircraft were kept busy carrying troops to trouble spots such as Cyprus, the Middle East and Borneo. From the bases, shorter-range aircraft would then deliver the troops to the front-line. And just as the Dakotas had dropped paratroops during the major operations of the war, so now the Beverleys, Argosys and Valettas dropped them in distant parts of the world.

But the short and medium range transports soon disappeared to be superseded by the aircraft that would take transport needs into the 21st Century - the giant Lockheed Hercules C-130.

their life early. Handley Page Victors were now chosen instead.

Refuelling also improved the RAF's reaction time. An entire Lightning squadron was deployed to the Far East, Tengah in Singapore, in the biggest refuelling exercise yet attempted.

Possibly the most famous long range trips were the bombing raids during the Falklands War. Codenamed Black Buck, the first operation involved 11 Victor tankers refuelling a single Vulcan during a 7,860 mile round trip from Ascension Island.

The coming of the jet age in the 1950s did not pass Transport Command by. The speed with which such aircraft could deliver a payload over long distances made the jet an attrac-

Victor BK.2 tanker at Jubail Air Base in Saudi Arabia after Operation Desert Storm on
3 March 1991

An international approach. An RAF RF-4 Phantom II moves in to refuel from a USAF KC-135 of
the 306th Strategic Refuelling Wing in September 1980

CHAPTER 42

THE MIGHTY 'HERC'

The Lockheed Hercules was originally built for the United States Air Force in the mid-fifties and had proved to be a reliable and robust aircraft. As the first Hercules were delivered to the RAF in 1966, the Americans were using them to great effect in resupplying troops in Vietnam.

Over 50 years in service the Hercules has been the most versatile aircraft in the RAF. Early versions carrying 99 troops have been stretched to take up to 128.

They can fly fully-loaded for 2500 miles and can deliver a bewildering range of stores and equipment. As the focus of military operations widened so the Hercules have been used many times to drop vitally-needed stores and food to starving populations in Africa and provide humanitarian relief around the world.

However the Hercules fleet, along with other transports in service, has been kept incredibly busy dealing with long military campaigns in Iraq and Afghanistan.

Final checks are underway before take off for an RAF C-130 Hercules taking part in the Rodeo 98 airlift competition at McChord AFB in Washington

CHAPTER 43

BUILDING A MODERN AIR FORCE

In 1969 Britain's strategic nuclear deterrent passed from the V-bombers of the RAF to nuclear submarines of the Royal Navy. From that point the RAF became primarily a tactical force geared towards the defence of Western Europe in association with the other armed services and those of Britain's allies.

In the event of conflict it was unlikely that either side would launch an immediate nuclear strike. Instead NATO's forces were geared to repulse a massive conventional Soviet attack into western Europe. RAF strategy and aircraft had evolved accordingly to meet this threat.

Britain's current nuclear deterrent, Trident, is carried by the Vigilant Class submarines. Here is HMS Victorious (04.04.2013)

SUPPORTING THE GROUND FORCES

In Europe the RAF was ready, together with its NATO allies, to take on any Soviet aggression directed from the heart of the Warsaw Pact countries.

If Soviet armour started rolling across the central European plains, NATO aircraft would have to stall the advance while reinforcements were rushed to the front line. They would hit key targets well behind the front line. Supply routes, truck and armoured vehicle parks, bridges and airfields would be attacked.

There was therefore a requirement for effective ground attack aircraft. Ideal in the role was the SEPECAT Jaguar, an Anglo-French collaboration, which had first entered service with the RAF in 1974. Using a system which guaranteed highly accurate navigation at low level the Jaguar was fast and excelled at delivering its weapons in one attack. The Jaguar squadrons spearheaded Britain's rapid reaction air force and as such were designed to operate from unprepared airfields and even stretches

A SEPECAT Jaguar ground attack fighter takes off. The Jaguar proved itself in the 1991 Gulf War

Two RAF Jaguar GR3As patrolling the Iraq no-fly zone during Operation Northern Watch in April 2002. They operated from Incirlik AFB in Turkey

of motorway in an emergency.

The Jaguar was joined in facing the Soviet threat by an aircraft with a truly revolutionary capability. The aircraft that added a new dimension to the service's Cold War capability was the Harrier. Developed by Hawker in the 1960s the GR1 entered squadron service in April 1969.

The Harrier was unique is its ability to take-off and land vertically as well as stop in midair. Key to this ability was its unique Rolls Royce Pegasus turbofan engine. This had four nozzles which could be vectored or swivelled to suit the particular flight condition. In practice, vertical take off used up valuable fuel and severely limited a useful payload, so pilots usually carried out a rolling take-off and landing.

In RAF Germany its mission was always close air support for the British Army. This meant that the Harriers could be based only minutes away from the ground forces it was supporting giving almost instant air cover.

A Harrier GR3 operating from woods in Germany in the early 1980s

CHAPTER 45

THE FALKLANDS WAR

The RAF was at a high state of readiness for an anticipated attack from the East but in 1982 Britain's forces were called to action in an entirely unexpected quarter.

On 2 April, Argentinian forces landed on the Falkland Islands, a British protectorate in the South Atlantic. Fighting a war 8,000 miles from Britain would primarily fall to the Royal Navy but such was the value attributed to air power that it fell to the RAF to demonstrate that a long-range attack could be mounted.

Operation Black Buck was designed to do precisely that. On 30 April a Vulcan dropped 21 1,000lb bombs on the airport runway at Port Stanley, the capital of the Falklands. After its sixth airborne refuelling from Victor tankers, the Vulcan completed what was then the longest bombing run in history, 7,860 miles, before it landed back at Ascension Island in the central Atlantic. Four further attacks took place over the next few weeks.

Although these strikes only had a short term effect on the capability of the airport they had a major effect on the deployment of enemy forces. They caused the Argentineans, fearing similar attacks on their capital, to pull their fighters back to defend Buenos Aires. This psychological victory heralded the start of the campaign to retake the Falklands.

With the nearest available British airfield over 3,000 miles away on

Most of the RAF helicopter force was lost when the SS Atlantic Conveyor sank while under tow after being hit by Argentinean Exocet missiles during the Falklands campaign in 1982

A Harrier GR3, the type operated by No.1 Squadron RAF during the Falklands War

Ascension Island carrier-based aircraft were the sole means of providing air power over the Falklands. Therefore vertical take off Harriers were the only option. The Fleet Air Arm operated Sea Harrier fighters as air defence over the task force while the RAF contributed No.1 Squadron's Harrier GR3 fighter bombers based on HMS Hermes.

Nimrods had two key maritime tasks during the war, to counter the threat posed by Argentinean submarines and to patrol the 200 miles exclusion zone that Britain had instigated round the islands.

Although the campaign to retake the Falklands was ultimately successful it was not without high cost. A number of Royal Navy ships were sunk mainly by Argentinean jets armed with French Exocet missiles that could be fired from many miles away. The lack of an airborne system warning of impending attack meant that these enemy jets could get through to the British ships virtually undetected. This lesson only served to reinforce the RAF's search for a replacement for the ageing Shackleton.

Operation Black Buck saw Vulcan bombers flying from Ascension Island to attack Port Stanley airport runway in the Falklands

CHAPTER 46

TORNADO STRIKE

In 1979 the RAF received the first examples of a new strike aircraft. The Tornado GR1 was to form the backbone of the RAF's frontline force. Developed jointly by Britain, Germany and Italy it was an advanced all-weather bomber. It had highly sophisticated electronic navigation and attack systems which allowed it to follow terrain automatically at low-level at high subsonic speeds.

The strike version was followed later in the 1980s by the Tornado fighter. The F.3 was a classic long range interceptor designed to replace the Phantoms and Lightnings that served the RAF for many years. Its role was to intercept enemy bombers and shoot them down if necessary.

By the end of the 1980s the RAF's front line reorganisation was almost complete. They were in good shape to continue their role defending Western Europe with their NATO allies. But in 1989 everything changed.

Three Panavia Tornado F.3 fighters in flight

An RAF Tornado GR4 takes off from Eilson AFB in Alaska during an exercise

CHAPTER 47

THE GULF WAR

The break up of the Soviet Union led to profound changes for NATO's defence policy. Almost overnight NATO's main enemy was seeking peace and the whole basis for the West's strategic thinking had become redundant. The British government sought to take advantage of the so-called peace dividend and drastically reduce its defence expenditure. Reductions were proposed that would cut the size of the RAF to its lowest level for 50 years. The document, called Options for Change, was presented to Parliament on 25 July 1990. One week later Iraq invaded Kuwait.

As the United Nations passed resolutions condemning the act of aggression British and American air bases prepared to rush reinforcements to Saudi Arabia and deter further incursions. The priority was to send fighters and airborne early warning aircraft.

The first aircraft to arrive in the Gulf on 7 August 1990 were AWACS and American F-15s. Four days later RAF Tornado F.3s landed at Dhahran in Saudi Arabia and immediately began flying combat air patrols along the Kuwait border

The American codename for this reinforcement was Operation Desert Shield. The RAF's contribution was Operation Granby.

The backbone of the RAF in the Gulf was the Tornado. The 18 F.3 fighters were joined by a formidable strike force of 62 GR1 bombers. Co-located with some of the Tornados at Muharraq in Bahrain was a detachment of 12 Jaguars which would provide battlefield air interdiction and support for the ground troops.

Tornado GR1 ZA447 was named 'Mig Eater' after destroying one on the ground during the Gulf War in 1991. Later it was found to have been a Mirage F.1

An RAF Tornado moves in to refuel from Victor K2 tanker XL164 'Saucy Sal'

Beginning as early as August 1990, Hercules of the Lyneham transport wing were involved in moving men and supplies as soon as the UK announced its intention to respond to the invasion of Kuwait.

Based in Saudi Arabia during the war, they were to carry nearly 14,000 passengers and 7,500,000 lbs of freight during the next few months. This ranged from military supplies such as ammunition and vehicles to post for the Desert Rats.

In December 1990 the United Nations passed a resolution to liberate Kuwait. When Iraq failed to comply with the UN's demands Desert Shield became Desert Storm.

The priority was to establish air superiority to provide an umbrella of friendly air cover. Then the strike aircraft could systematically destroy the Iraqi war machine. The first targets were radar, guns and missile installations as well as the Iraqi air force. The whole array of command and control centres such as military headquarters, communications and supply routes were vital targets. Iraqi forces would not be allowed to respond.

Tornado crew Jon Peters and John Nichol, fit and healthy, after their XV Squadron Tornado GR1 was shot down on an ultra low-level runway busting operation.. Both survived capture and torture in Iraq

Three Buccaneers flying direct from Lossiemouth to Muharraq in Bahrain photographed from their Tristar tanker. It was 10 February 1991 and day 26 of the Gulf War

At 01.30 on 17 January 1991 Toma-hawk cruise missiles were fired from US Navy warships in the Persian Gulf. They were followed by wave after wave of Coalition bombers hitting radar stations and communications. 2,000 targets were hit in the first ten minutes.

The RAF Tornado bombers had a special task in this vast scenario. They were to fly in at ultra low level and destroy Iraq's airfields using the runway-busting JP233 bombs. But this operation required the aircraft to directly overfly the target. Carried out at night most of the Tornado attacks were successful despite intense flak and surface to air missiles. However such was the scale of the enemy defences three Tornados were

shot down in three successive nights.

Day four of the campaign brought a switch of tactics. The Tornados went to medium level attacks flying at around 10,000 ft using freefall bombs against airfields and other targets. Playing a largely unsung combat support role the Victor, VC10 and Tristar tankers

The workhorse of the war. An RAF Hercules carries more troops to the front

were essential to the British war effort. Each heavily-armed Tornado needed two refuellings on the way to its target and one on the way back. This meant that the tankers had to fly near or even in Iraqi air space to wait for the returning Tornados.

One of the true success stories of Desert Storm was the use of precision guided munitions. Back at home viewers watching the war on television were stunned by the accuracy with which these weapons could hit a target apparently without any damage to the surrounding area.

RAF Tornados began to drop laser-guided bombs, or LGBs, on 2 February 1991, over two weeks into the campaign. LGBs detected the splash of laser light reflected off the target, a light that came from an airborne laser designator.

Providing the service initially for the Tornado force was the veteran Buccaneer. The Tornado - Buccaneer duo became deadly hitting bridges, hardened aircraft shelters and even Iraqi runways with unerring accuracy.

Eight days later the Tornado force became operational with its own airborne laser designator, the GEC Marconi TIALD pod, or Thermal Imaging Airborne Laser Designator.

Once air superiority had been established RAF Jaguars attacked the Iraqi army in Kuwait blowing up ammunition and fuel dumps, tanks and missile sites. At 04.00 on 24 February ground troops moved in. The land campaign was swift, around 100 hours. The Iraqi army surrendered. Kuwait had been liberated.

There were many lessons to be learned from the Gulf War but in the light of overwhelming success military commanders warned against seizing obvious but possibly misleading conclusions which might be applied to future conflicts. Coalition forces had six months to train and prepare for war. They would not always have this luxury in the future. The RAF had lost six Tornados and, while the runway busting bombs had proved effective, it still seemed a high price to pay for success. However the Jaguars had flown 600 combat sorties and not a single aircraft had been lost. They had played a significant role in destroying huge amounts of Iraqi armour and artillery.

An RAF Jaguar GR1A being serviced on the flight line at Muharraq during Operation Desert Shield on 23 January 1991

CHAPTER 48

OPERATIONS IN THE BALKANS

The need for increased flexibility was one of the key lessons of the Gulf War for the RAF and it would not be long before the lessons learned in the Gulf War were put to good use.

In 1993 the United Nations ordered the policing of the skies over Bosnia-Herzogovina, an independent state recreated after the break-up of Yugoslavia, which had descended into civil war. As part of Operation Deny Flight Jaguars and Tornado F.3s flew over Bosnia from their base in Southern Italy denying the Serbian aggressors the ability to launch their aircraft against Bosnian targets. Most important in the operation was the Boeing E-3D Sentry. Based on the old Boeing 707 airframe, and sporting a massive AWACS dish, they provided a much improved early warning capability than that of the Shackletons which had now been retired.

Sentries clocked up over 9,000 hours in surveillance of the skies over Bosnia. Nimrods patrolled the waters of the Adriatic sea to enforce the trade embargo and tankers provided the much needed refuelling capabilities.

By the summer of 1995, after yet another abortive ceasefire, the continued slaughter of civilians and even the hijacking of United Nations equipment, NATO took direct action against the Serbs with Operation Deliberate Force. Serb gun positions, ammunition depots and communications installations were the targets of precision bombing.

The Boeing E-3D Sentry was a vital element of control for the war in the Balkans

Once again laser guided bombs showed their value at taking out key targets.

After this NATO intervention an uneasy peace descended on the region.

The war in Bosnia was not the only action in the Balkans that involved the RAF, Ethnic conflict reared its ugly head in Kosovo and the UN was determined there would be no repeat of the earlier genocide in the Balkans. In May 1999 NATO forces in the Mediterranean and Europe launched a sustained bombing strike against Yugoslav military targets in retaliation for the Yugoslavian refusal to abide by the agreements made over Kosovo the previous year. RAF Harriers of No.1 Squadron and Tristar tankers operating from Italian airfields took part in the campaign which had the full support of all the NATO member countries. RAF Tornados also joined the attack which continued through May. On 4 June the Serbian parliament accepted a G8 peace agreement and on 10 June NATO called a halt to the bombing. The airstrikes had done their job.

In 2001 the terrorist attack on the World Trade Centre changed the face of global security. As a result Operation Enduring Freedom was launched against the Taliban in Afghanistan. The RAF was heavily involved in the campaign. Canberra PR9s undertook photo reconnaissance missions, Nimrods patrolled the Gulf and surrounding areas and Sentry E-3Ds took part in AWACS coverage in the area. The Joint Helicopter Force also supplied vital support for the troops on the ground flying in very difficult conditions and in mountainous terrain. 99 Squadron had only just taken delivery of four Boeing C-17s. These were deployed almost immediately, together with Hercules, to provide essential airlift capability. With a payload of almost 75 tons it carries nearly four times as much as the Hercules but with a similar performance.

An RAF Nimrod R1 of 51 Squadron which provided signals intelligence for allied forces in many operations

CHAPTER 49

BACK TO IRAQ

But the largest commitment was to Operation Telic in 2003, the attack on Iraq. The RAF already had 25 aircraft and 1,000 personnel in the area to support the no-fly zone imposed on Iraqi President, Saddam Hussein. During the operation a further 100 aircraft were deployed together with 7,000 personnel. The deployment included Tornado GR4s and Harrier GR7s in the attack role together with a full range of aircraft in air defence and support.

As the 'shock and awe' air campaign began hundreds of sorties were flown every day with the RAF making a significant contribution. They flew almost 1,400 offensive strikes, most with precision munitions. It also saw the first operation for the new Storm Shadow stand off precision air-to-ground missile dropped by Tornado GR4s of 617 Squadron. It is designed to attack important hardened targets

RAF personnel board a C-17 Globemaster for one of its regular flights from Kandahar Airfield to the UK during the war in Afghanistan (13.11.2014)

A Tornado GR4 of 617 Squadron fitted with a Storm Shadow cruise missile under the fuselage (01.02.2004)

such as buried command centres.

Saddam's regime fell but that was not the end of RAF operations in the area.

Since that time seldom has a day gone by when RAF aircraft have not taken on a vital operation in support of British, NATO or UN activities somewhere around the world. In the last ten years alone they have been involved with the military intervention in Libya, humanitarian relief after the Pakistan earthquake of 2005, operations in Iraq until withdrawal in 2011, assisting with the Ebola virus outbreak in West Africa, the war in Afghanistan which continued until 2014, helping the search for kidnapped children in Nigeria, the NATO policing mission in the Baltic States and, of course, the ongoing fight against ISIL in parts of Iraq.

Add to these their day to day duties of defending the UK and her bases abroad, and the ongoing presence in the Persian Gulf it has been and continues to be an extremely busy time for a slimmed down service.

Slimmed down is perhaps an understatement considering that the number of RAF personnel has dropped from approximately 88,000 at the time of the Gulf War in 1991 to an approximate 35,000 25 years later. It is hard to judge effectiveness as different aircraft are involved, there are more joint operations with the other armed services, many responsibilities are undertaken by the private sector and, perhaps most changed of all, the potential enemies are very different.

One thing, however, that does not change is the professional way the RAF goes about training its personnel.

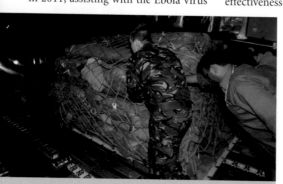
RAF personnel unload humanitarian aid for Pakistan's flood victims from a C-17 (08.08.2010)

21st Century operations for the RAF. A Tornado GR4 armed with Paveway IV prepares for a mission over Libya (25.05.2011) (top); a Chinook over Afghan mountains (25.03.2015) (centre right); a 33 Squadron Puma deploys flares during Operation Toral in Afghanistan (14.12.2015); and a VC10 C.1K tanker from 101 Squadron undergoes maintenance during the 2003 Iraq war

CHAPTER 50

TRAINING FOR THE MODERN RAF

What has become clear for the RAF is that its ability to fight at short notice in any location is paramount. To maintain this capability the RAF depends on the skills of their pilots. They are trained for every eventuality and Cranwell is where that training starts.

Cranwell has been the RAF's officer cadet college since 1920. Thousands of would-be pilots have taken the training course there but only the few go on to gain that most coveted of symbols, their wings.

In the beginning basic flying training was on the Avro 504 and later the Tiger Moth and the Chipmunk. Now the prospective pilot learns on the Grob Tutor. The first few hours will be just as demanding and terrifying as they were for the thousands of young cadets before.

ATA ferry pilots being trained on Tiger Moths at Hatfield before the Second World War

Avro 504s used to train RFC and RAF pilots during the First World War

Having learned basic navigation and control of piston-engined aircraft the cadet progresses to ab initio training on the Shorts Tucano. The Tucano provides the pilot with their first taste of what it might be like to fly in an aircraft with a cockpit configured like a fighter. The Tucano is an ideal aircraft for this role as it has similar jet flight flying characteristics as the BAe Systems Hawk, the RAF's advanced jet trainer.

If the student pilot makes the grade he or she will progress to RAF Valley in North Wales. There they will be introduced to the Hawk. This aircraft gives the pilot the opportunity to not only develop the skills needed to fly a fast jet but also to learn how to fight in one.

A BAE Systems Hawk, the fast jet trainer for the RAF for more than 40 years

Short Tucano ZF135 delivered to the RAF in 1986

CHAPTER 51

THE RED ARROWS

The RAF still needs to show the public that their money is well spent and as commitments round the globe increase there is less opportunity for the full range of front line aircraft to be displayed.

However one area of RAF expertise has now been around for more than 50 years. The Red Arrows were formed in 1964 and displayed for the first time as a team in 1965. They flew one of the main training aircraft of the day, the Folland Gnat, and became instant air show favourites. In 1980 they converted to the latest RAF jet trainer, the Hawk, which has been their aircraft of choice ever since.

After almost 5,000 displays the Red Arrows are acknowledged as the world's finest display team. However not only do they perform for the public all over the world, they also provide a vital service supporting the British aviation industry in the search for important export orders and promoting innovation and technology. As recent as 2016 they flew a major Far East tour visiting 17 countries including China for the first time.

The Red Arrows have spectacularly represented the RAF and British industry for more than 50 years

CHAPTER 52

THE 21ST CENTURY RAF

When fully qualified pilots complete their training the RAF of which they become an integral part is a very different one from that of just a few years ago.

Gone are the Harrier, the Jaguar and the Tornado F.3.

Gone too are the Nimrods, swept away in 2010 when the proposed new MRA4 variant was cancelled and the existing aircraft scrapped. By then the last few remaining Canberra PR9s, the longest serving aircraft in RAF history, had also been retired. Virtually the entire long-serving tanker fleet of VC10s and Tristars has also gone.

In their place is a very different and exciting organisation.

A Typhoon FGR4 with pilot in full flying kit in Latvia (17.02.2016)

The RAFs Hercules fleet have provided a constant heavy lift, troop carrying and casevac capability for more than 50 years. Here a 47 Squadron C-130J is seen near the Welsh coast (01.09.2015)

CHAPTER 53

RAF PRESENT AND FUTURE

On the frontline is the Eurofighter Typhoon. Original models were pure air defence fighters but these F.2 aircraft soon became true multi role aircraft hence the change to FGR4 reflecting their ground attack and reconnaissance roles. The cause

An RAF Airbus A400M Atlas, described as a tactical airlifter with strategic capabilities, has been in service since 2013 (05.02.2015)

of much speculation in the beginning due to a lack of vector thrust and stealth characteristics the Typhoon has proved itself on operations since its introduction in 2003.

The Tornado GR4 is still the strike aircraft of choice but now using a

bewildering array of weaponry from the tried and tested Storm Shadow and Brimstone to a range of Paveway LGBs and missiles.

For intelligence gathering and command and control the RAF continues to operate the E-3D Sentry which has been joined by the Sentinel R1, a Bombardier Global Express executive jet converted by Raytheon that provides ground surveillance. The Beechcraft Super King Air, known as the Shadow R1 in the RAF, operates in the ISTAR role, intelligence, surveillance, target acquisition and reconnaissance. The latest additions are Boeing RC-135 'Rivet Joint' reconnaissance aircraft based on the long-serving C-135 US Air Force airframes.

The most recent variant of the Hercules, the C-130J, is still the RAF's key tactical transport while the C-17 Globemaster III is the strategic long-range airlifter. Latest transport in the fleet, however, is the Airbus A400M 'Atlas' which will replace the ageing C-130J

Design & Artwork: ALEX YOUNG

Published by: DEMAND MEDIA LIMITED

Publishers: JASON FENWICK

Written by: COLIN HIGGS

in the long term.

The tanker responsibilities for the next 30 years are now in the hands of another Airbus aircraft, the converted A330-200 now known as 'Voyager'. Designated as MRTT the name accurately reflects its varied abilities, Multi Role Tanker Transport.

The long term future of the RAF and Fleet Air Arm rests heavily with the Lockheed Martin F-35B Lightning II, a multi role flexible STOVL combat aircraft (07.2016)

However going forward there will be some major additions to this list.

The Boeing P-8 Poseidon will fill the maritime patrol gap left by the scrapping of Nimrod.

There will be new Typhoon squadrons as the Tornado GR4 is finally phased out.

The RAF's first foray into unmanned aerial vehicle technology with the MQ-9 Reaper will be extended as they begin to test future home-grown UAVs.

There will be a wholesale replacement of training aircraft as well but one name stands out as being an aircraft that the RAF will rely on for the foreseeable future.

The Lockheed Martin F-35 Lightning II will bring back vertical and short take off capabilities to both the RAF and Royal Navy for the first time since the demise of the Harriers. It is described as a fifth generation fighter which means that it will be stealthy, have high performance and be packed with the very latest electronics for finding, targeting and destroying the enemy all in a supersonic package.

Only time will tell if this mix of tried and tested and new and exciting will fit the bill but it ensures the future of the independent RAF into the future.

A Sentinel R.1, Raytheon's conversion of a Bombardier Global Express, provides battlefield and ground surveillance

An MQ-9 Reaper UAV which was introduced in 2007. In the Afghanistan conflict Reaper flew more than 71,000 hours on operations providing intelligence and reconnaisance but with a deadly weapon capability if required